Just Enough
SPANISH
GRAMMAR
Illustrated

Gabriele Stobbe

New York   Chicago   San Francisco   Lisbon   London   Madrid   Mexico City
Milan   New Delhi   San Juan   Seoul   Singapore   Sydney   Toronto

Library of Congress Cataloging-in-Publication Data

Stobbe, Gabriele
    Just enough Spanish grammar illustrated / Gabriele Stobbe.
        p.   cm. — (Just enough)
        ISBN 0-07-149233-X (alk. paper)
        1. Spanish language—Grammar.   2. Spanish language—Textbooks for
foreign speakers—English.   I. Title.

PC4112.S76   2007
468.2′421—dc22   2007019652

To my son, Alexis George Stobbe,
whose support and unshakeable belief in my talents
assisted me in realizing my vision

The author also thanks Meaghan McLean (www.subscriptionart.com) for designing
the wonderful graphic illustrations that bring the book to life; Kimberly Werner
(www.DesignInterventionPA.com) for adding her artistic touch to the project; Beulah Hager
for proofreading the manuscript; Perry Meyer and Anna South for assistance with the
English text; and Cynthia Lennox, ESL professor at Duquesne University, for her suggestions
and feedback.

1 2 3 4 5 6 7 8 9 0 CTPS/CTPS 0 9 8 7

ISBN   978-0-07-149233-1
MHID   0-07-149233-X

Also available in this series: Just Enough English Grammar Illustrated

McGraw-Hill books are available at special quantity discounts to use as premiums and
sales promotions, or for use in corporate training programs. For more information, please
write to the Director of Special Sales, Professional Publishing, McGraw-Hill, Two Penn
Plaza, New York, NY 10121-2298. Or contact your local bookstore.

This book is printed on acid-free paper.

CONTENTS

Introduction
v

Nouns
1

Adjectives
33

Pronouns
69

Verbs
101

Adverbs
149

Prepositions
155

Conjunctions
167

Interjections
171

Answer Key
176

INTRODUCTION

What This Book Contains

■ *Just Enough Spanish Grammar Illustrated* requires no formal exposure to Spanish grammar. The book is designed to give learners of Spanish a basic grammar foundation. It may serve other students as a reference or review tool.

■ This book takes a practical approach. It does not focus on rules and definitions. Instead, it studies how words work and what they do in sentences.

The material is presented in an easy, step-by-step format. As the learner moves through the book, he or she will gain an understanding of the basic principles of the Spanish language. These principles are laid out simply but thoroughly, and each new principle builds on what the student learned earlier in the book.

■ Real-life scenarios use interesting characters and engaging, simple vocabulary. Basic Spanish structures presented in visually engaging graphics bring grammar alive and therefore increase the student's desire to learn grammar.

■ Carefully designed graphic illustrations translate grammatical concepts into visual images. Each topic or grammar concept is clearly explained with relevant graphic illustrations. They make comprehension possible without wordy explanations.

■ Graphic organizers clarify concepts and help the reader review. They stimulate creative and logical thought processes, and also help the student to evaluate and categorize language structures.

■ Review Exercises and an Answer Key provide the learner with the opportunity to test his or her skills.

■ This book offers choices. It takes into account the different ways in which students learn and, accordingly, provides a variety of learning tools. From real-life scenarios to illustrations and graphic organizers, there is something for everyone.

Organization of Chapters

Your Framework

The eight chapters of this book are organized around the eight parts of speech. It is important to become familiar with the name of each part of speech and to expand your knowledge about each one. The parts of speech will become the overall framework of your Spanish language knowledge. It is to this framework that you will add important information necessary to build your basic grammar foundation.

The following strategies were designed to show you how the eight parts of speech can help you to build your foundation.

Your Strategies: Words Are Tools for Communication

Strategy #1: How to Use Your Tools

Becoming familiar with your tools is the first strategy. Words are tools for communication. The vocabulary words used in this book were chosen because of their applicability to real-life scenarios. Your tools—Spanish vocabulary words with their matching English definitions—are at the end of this Introduction. The first vocabulary list introduces the players; the second list contains words reflecting the pool theme. The players represented throughout the book are everyday people. They add a new, refreshing approach to what is usually dry material. You will find illustrations of all key players, followed by brief biographies of the main personalities. The final progress check is based on these biographies.

With the needs of beginning Spanish language learners in mind, common words that translate into powerful graphic images have been selected. These words and images should help you understand the essential grammar concepts in which the words appear.

Strategy #2: Basic Language Concept Number One: Form of the Eight Parts of Speech

Most of the chapters in this book are divided into two parts. Typically, the part of speech that is the focus of the chapter is first discussed in terms of its *form*—the qualities that it has in common with other parts of speech. Then the *use* of each part of speech is considered.

What Information Do All of These Parts of Speech Give?

In this book, you will learn about three important concepts: number, gender, and grammar person. Part One of several of the chapters will show how these three concepts are expressed in the different parts of speech.

Strategy #3: Basic Language Concept Number Two: Use of the Eight Parts of Speech

What Jobs Can All of These Parts of Speech Do?

Part Two will build on what you learn in Part One. In many chapters, Part Two explains the jobs that different parts of speech perform in a sentence, as well as the relationships between different words within a sentence. A thorough understanding of the concepts covered in Part One will make Part Two seem much easier!

Strategy #4: Details About Chapter Sequence: Understanding the Framework of the Book

At the end of each chapter, you will find a section titled "Details About Chapter Sequence." In this section, we tell you how the order of the chapters relates to your learning process. This section is yet another tool to enhance your knowledge.

Your Players: Family and Friends

The Miller Family

Mr. Miller	Mrs. Miller	Anna Miller	Andy Miller
father	**mother**	**daughter**	**son**

the parents

Anna	Andy
sister	**brother**

Lakeside Pool Friends

Ben	Jake	Susan	Maria	Anna
the boy	**the boy**	**the girl**	**the girl**	**the girl**

the boys   the girls

Kelly	Andy	Charles Smith	Mrs. Miller
the young girl	**the young boy**	**the man**	**the woman**

the children   the pool manager   the teacher

Your Players: Family and Friends

La familia Miller

señor Miller	señora Miller	Anna Miller	Andy Miller
el padre	**la madre**	**la hija**	**el hijo**

los padres

Anna	Andy
la hermana	**el hermano**

Los amigos de la piscina

Ben	Jake	Susan	Maria	Anna
el chico	**el chico**	**la chica**	**la chica**	**la chica**

los chicos   **las chicas**

Kelly	Andy	Charles Smith	señora Miller
la niña	**el niño**	**el hombre**	**la mujer**

los niños   **el gerente de la piscina**   **la maestra**

Your Tools: English Vocabulary Words

bikini

locker room

towel

life preserver

beach ball

suntan lotion

sunglasses

pool

flippers

umbrella

bathing suit

lifeguard chair

Mexican hat

air mattress

diving board

whistle

pool ladder

hamburger

hot dog

goggles

Your Tools: Spanish Vocabulary Words

el bikini

el vestuario

la toalla

el salvavidas

la pelota

la crema
de sol

los anteojos
de sol

la piscina

las aletas
de buceo

el parasol

el traje
de baño

la silla
de Susan

el sombrero

el colchón
de aire

el trampolín

el silbato

la escalera

la hamburguesa

el perro
caliente

las gafas
de piscina

MEET THE PLAYERS

Susan

Susan vive en Miami, Florida. Tiene 16 años.
Susan tiene un hermano. Su nombre es Tim.
Ella tiene un gato. Su gato se llama Snowball.
Su gato es pequeño. Susan ama a su gato.

Maria

Maria es estudiante de intercambio. Es de Mexico.
Tiene 16 años. Ella vive con Anna y su familia.
Está contenta en los Estados Unidos. Habla bien
el inglés. Maria y Anna hablan español.

Ben

Ben vive en Miami. Tiene 17 años. Ben tiene una
hermana. Su hermana se llama Claire. Ben tiene
un perro. Su perro es inteligente. Se llama Shadow.
Ben tiene muchos amigos.

Anna

Anna vive en Miami. Es de Seattle. Ella tiene
16 años. Las amigas de Anna son Susan y Maria.
El hermano de Anna se llama Andy. La madre
de Anna es maestra. Anna ama a su mamá.
Anna habla español lentamente.

Jake

Jake es el rival de Ben. Él tiene 18 años. Jake
tiene dos hermanos. Sus hermanos se llaman
Frank y Ryan.

CHAPTER 1

NOUNS

PART ONE: FORM OF SPANISH NOUNS

1.1 What Is a Noun? 2

1.2 Number of Spanish Nouns 2

1.3 Gender of Spanish Nouns 4

1.4 Spanish Noun Endings 7

1.5 Spanish Nouns and Articles 9

PART TWO: USES OF SPANISH NOUNS

1.6 Nouns as Subjects 17

1.7 Nouns Showing Possession 21

1.8 When Verbs Expand to Include Objects: Direct Objects 23

1.9 Another Type of Object: Objects of Prepositions 27

1.10 Details About Chapter Sequence 29

1.11 Overview of Spanish Nouns 30

1.12 Spanish Noun Practice 32

PART ONE: FORM OF SPANISH NOUNS
What Information Do Nouns Give?

1.1 What Is a Noun?

A noun is one of the most important words you use when speaking and writing. A noun tells whom or what you are talking about.

> A ***noun*** **is a word used to name a person, place, thing, or idea.**

Maria
Maria

señora Miller
Mrs. Miller

el niño
the boy

la pelota
the ball

la piscina
the pool

el sombrero
the hat

la escuela
the school

! Hint: Rules for capitalization of Spanish nouns are not always the same as those for English nouns. Watch out for this as you progress.

1.2 Number of Spanish Nouns

Nouns carry information about number. When a noun refers to one person or thing, it is *singular* in number. When it refers to more than one of the same type of thing, it is *plural* in number.

One   More Than One

Singular   Plural

**The number of a noun is indicated by its ending.
The final letters of a noun determine
how its plural is formed.**

The following examples illustrate how to change from the
singular form of a noun to its plural form.

Singular   Plural

la pelota   las pelotas

The plural of most Spanish nouns is formed by adding -s when
the noun ends in a vowel: **a, e, i, o,** or **u.**

el parasol   los parasoles

Nouns ending in the consonants **l, r,** or **n** form their plurals
by adding **-es.**

el salvavidas   los salvavidas

Nouns ending in the consonant **s** remain the same in the plural.

el lápiz   los lápices

Nouns ending in the consonant **z** form the plural by changing **z**
to **c** and adding **-es.**

Throughout this book we use the term *building block* to
illustrate basic concepts of the Spanish language. When you use
a noun as a building block, you must first determine if it is a
singular or a plural noun. As you progress, you will learn how
to add words to the noun to form sentences. It is your basic
building block. The form of the words you add to the noun
depends on the information the noun gives you.

3

Here are two examples of nouns that have been extended by adding a verb to show what kind of verb follows the noun.

In the first example, a singular noun is connected to a singular verb form in order to say *the beach umbrella is*. In the second example, we added a plural verb form to say *the beach umbrellas are*.

Examples:

parasol es

Singular Noun   Singular Verb Form

parasoles son

Plural Noun   Plural Verb Form

It is not always easy for beginners to recognize or use plural noun forms. But as the examples above show, stringing words together to make a sentence requires you to apply the concept of number to the words you are using. This is the first step toward forming a grammatically correct sentence.

1.3 Gender of Spanish Nouns

The second step toward forming a correct sentence is recognizing the gender of nouns. When you talk about a boy, you are referring to a person who is male; *boy* is a *masculine* noun. Likewise, when you talk about a girl, you are talking about a person who is female; *girl* is a *feminine* noun. In English, the gender of many nouns is based on their biological nature.

Other nouns, like *hat, chair,* and *book* pictured here, show no clear gender. Nouns with no clear gender are thought of as being *neuter,* neither masculine nor feminine. In grammar, the distinction between masculine, feminine, and neuter nouns is called *gender.*

Here is an illustration of Ben and Susan. *Ben* is an example of a masculine noun, while *Susan* is an example of a feminine noun.

Ben
Masculine

Susan
Feminine

Male
Masculine

Female
Feminine

Throughout this book, the male symbol indicates that the noun is masculine. The female symbol is used for nouns that are feminine.

Nouns carry information about gender.

In general, English nouns fall into one of three categories: masculine, feminine, or neuter. However, the Spanish language divides nouns into only two groups: masculine nouns and feminine nouns. The following chart contrasts the gender of English nouns and the gender of Spanish nouns.

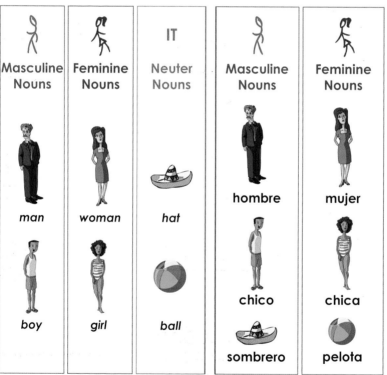

In Spanish, nouns that name inanimate objects are either masculine or feminine, just like nouns for people.

In the chart above, we use the symbols for male and female to indicate the gender of a noun for people in both English and Spanish. Note that in Spanish, the symbols are used for inanimate objects as well.

Symbols for Inanimate Objects

 **Masculine**   **Feminine**

el sombrero	el silbato	la crema	la pelota
Masculine Noun	Masculine Noun	Feminine Noun	Feminine Noun

All Spanish nouns are either masculine or feminine in gender, whether they are persons or things.

! *Hint: Be prepared for some memorization. You must learn each noun as either masculine or feminine. There are no shortcuts!*

Let's take a closer look at the concept of number again. The following chart shows plural forms of nouns together with the gender symbols.

Plural Spanish Nouns

6

We have stated that a noun is your basic building block and that it carries information about number and gender. For Spanish nouns, number and gender go together. You can't separate one from the other. For the beginner, this means that you must find out if the noun is singular or plural (number). Next, find out if the noun is masculine or feminine (gender). Once you know both of these things about a noun, you can expand your building block.

Consider the following example to see how we added other words to **Estados** (*States*).

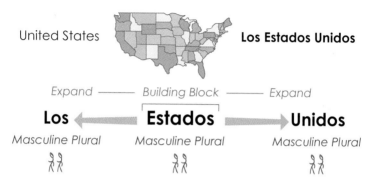

United States

Los Estados Unidos

Expand ——— Building Block ——— Expand

Los ← **Estados** → **Unidos**

Masculine Plural   Masculine Plural   Masculine Plural

Can you predict that any matching verb must be in plural form? If you can, you are on your way to understanding that all building blocks must match in order to form a sentence correctly.

Hint: Become a "Match Wizard"! This will add fun to the task of memorizing Spanish nouns. Be smart and recognize that no one can memorize them for you. Make it a game!

1.4 Spanish Noun Endings

In general, endings indicate the gender of Spanish nouns. However, the basic rules are not always a safe way to determine gender for a noun. There are many exceptions to these basic rules that will make your task of learning gender by noun endings more challenging.

Dictionaries and language textbooks indicate the gender of Spanish nouns, using *m.* for masculine or *f.* for feminine after each entry.

The following illustrations give a short summary of common exceptions for masculine and feminine nouns.

Most Masculine Nouns End in -o

el amigo
friend (male)

el hijo
son

el libro
book

el chico
boy

el niño
young boy

Exceptions: Masculine Nouns That End in -a

el día
day

el idioma
language

el clima
climate

Most Feminine Nouns End in -a

la amiga
friend (female)

la hija
daughter

la escuela
school

la niña
young girl

Exceptions: Feminine Nouns That End in -o

la mano
hand

la radio
radio

la foto
photograph

Exceptions:

Feminine Nouns That End in -d

la nacionalidad
nationality

Feminine Nouns That End in -ión

la lección
lesson

Other nouns can be either masculine or feminine. In such cases, the word that shows whether the noun is being used as a masculine or a feminine noun is called the *article*. Articles will be covered in the next section. For now, know that **el** (*the*) placed before a noun indicates a masculine word and **la** (*the*) indicates a feminine word.

el estudiante *(male student)*	**la estudiante** *(female student)*
el joven *(young man)*	**la joven** *(young woman)*
el artista *(male artist)*	**la artista** *(female artist)*

! *Hint: Learn each noun's gender **individually**—your efforts will pay off!*

1.5 Spanish Nouns and Articles

Spanish nouns are accompanied by other words called *articles,* which are placed before the noun; articles add details about the noun that follows. Another grammar term to learn with articles is the verb *to modify.* Modifying a noun means giving more information about the noun or qualifying it.

> **An article is placed *before* a noun and signals that a noun follows. It gives information about the number and gender of the noun it modifies.**

There are two basic groups of articles. One group, the *indefinite articles,* indicates that the noun refers to any member of a group, or to a person or thing in general. The second group, the *definite articles,* indicates that the noun refers to a specific or particular person or thing.

Overview of Article Charts

The following charts show the correct use of articles.

Spanish Definite Articles: People
Spanish Indefinite Articles: Symbols
Spanish Definite Articles: People and Things
Spanish Indefinite Articles: Symbols and Things

Spanish Definite Articles: People

Definite Article	Noun	Grammar Details
el *the*	chico *boy*	The definite article **el** adds details about the noun **chico**. Use this article with a masculine singular noun.
la *the*	chica *girl*	The definite article **la** adds details about the noun **chica**. Use this article with a feminine singular noun.
los *the*	chicos *boys*	The definite article **los** adds details about the noun **chicos**. Use this article with a masculine plural noun.
las *the*	chicas *girls*	The definite article **las** adds details about the noun **chicas**. Use this article with a feminine plural noun.

Spanish Indefinite Articles: Symbols

Indefinite Article	Noun	Grammar Details
un *a*	chico *boy*	The indefinite article **un** adds details about the noun **chico**. Use this article with a masculine singular noun. **Un chico** can also be translated as *one boy*.
una *a*	chica *girl*	The indefinite article **una** adds details about the noun **chica**. Use this article with a feminine singular noun. **Una chica** can also be translated as *one girl*.
unos *some*	chicos *boys*	The indefinite article **unos** adds details about the noun **chicos**. Use this article with a masculine plural noun. **Unos chicos** can also be translated as *a few boys*.
unas *some*	chicas *girls*	The indefinite article **unas** adds details about the noun **chicas**. Use this article with a feminine plural noun. **Unas chicas** can also be translated as *a few girls*.

The gender symbols represent the information expressed by the article.

Spanish Definite Articles: People and Things

	People	*Things*
Masculine Nouns	**el chico** *the boy*	**el sombrero** *the hat*
	los chicos *the boys*	**los sombreros** *the hats*

	People	*Things*
Feminine Nouns	**la chica** *the girl*	**la pelota** *the ball*
	las chicas *the girls*	**las pelotas** *the balls*

In this chart, people and things are combined. The articles for inanimate objects follow the same pattern of number and gender as the articles for people.

Spanish Indefinite Articles: Symbols and Things

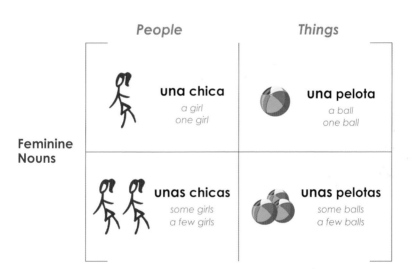

	People	Things
Masculine Nouns	**un chico** *a boy / one boy*	**un sombrero** *a hat / one hat*
	unos chicos *some boys / a few boys*	**unos sombreros** *some hats / a few hats*

	People	Things
Feminine Nouns	**una chica** *a girl / one girl*	**una pelota** *a ball / one ball*
	unas chicas *some girls / a few girls*	**unas pelotas** *some balls / a few balls*

**A Spanish article must match the noun it modifies
both in gender and in number.
Use the article to identify the gender of a noun.**

You must first determine whether a noun is masculine or
feminine. Next, determine whether it is singular or plural.
Remember, it is a matching game!

*! Hint: For a beginner, recognizing the differences between
singular and plural nouns is not always easy. There are many
rules to observe. Be patient! Keep practicing, and this skill
will come naturally.*

Here is a short English sentence to show you how widely used
articles are.

Example:

Book belongs to teacher.

You could improve the correctness of this sentence by adding the
missing articles: ***The*** *book belongs to* ***the*** *teacher.*

**The form of a Spanish noun, based on number and
gender, determines many other parts in a sentence.**

*! Hint: Looking at simple sentences will greatly enhance your
comprehension as you learn basic structures.*

Let's review two previous examples from this chapter and
add missing articles, verbs, and adjectives to build a sentence.
Use the arrow ⬇ over the noun as your starting point.

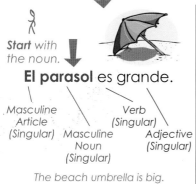

Start with
the noun. ⬇

El parasol es grande.

Masculine   Verb
Article   (Singular)
(Singular)   Masculine   Adjective
       Noun   (Singular)
       (Singular)

The beach umbrella is big.

Start with
the noun. ⬇

Los parasoles son grandes.

Masculine   Masculine   Verb   Adjective
Article   Noun   (Plural)   (Plural)
(Plural)   (Plural)

The beach umbrellas are big.

In the first example, the definite article **el** provides details about the noun **parasol**. Since **el** is singular and masculine, like the noun it modifies, you can predict that the adjective **grande** will be singular and masculine as well. You can also predict that the verb that relates to **el parasol**—**es**—will be singular.

Like **el**, the definite article **los** provides details about the noun it modifies. If you know that **los** is plural and masculine, you can predict that **grandes**, the adjective that follows, will also be plural and masculine. You will also know that the verb—**son**—will be plural.

Hint: Recognize the value of learning to make matches early on. The process of matching the components of a sentence in gender and number starts with nouns.

The following examples will help you to analyze the article **la** step-by-step.

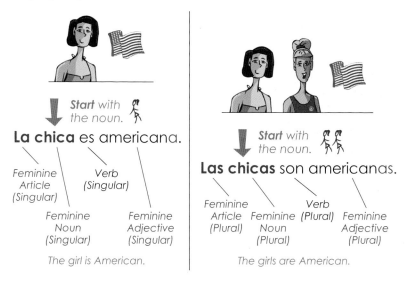

La chica es americana.

Feminine Article (Singular)

Verb (Singular)

Feminine Noun (Singular)

Feminine Adjective (Singular)

Start with the noun.

The girl is American.

Las chicas son americanas.

Start with the noun.

Feminine Article (Plural)

Feminine Noun (Plural)

Verb (Plural)

Feminine Adjective (Plural)

The girls are American.

In the first example, the definite article **la** provides details about the noun **chica**. If you analyze **la** for gender and number, you find that it is feminine and singular. It matches **chica**, the noun it modifies.

This pattern of matching gender and number can be repeated with the adjective and the verb. If you look at the adjective and the verb in each of the sentences above, you find the word singular or plural below each one.

Americana is a feminine adjective in singular form.
Americanas is a feminine adjective in plural form. Can you predict the form of the verb? The verbs are also marked as singular or plural: The verb **es** is a singular verb; the verb **son** is a plural verb.

All of the components together form a sentence in which everything matches.

> **Articles express gender and number through their form. They are placed before a noun. The noun that follows matches the article in gender and number.**

Let's summarize the use of definite articles:

the man

el: masculine singular article + **hombre**: masculine singular noun

the men

los: masculine plural article + **hombres**: masculine plural noun

the woman

la: feminine singular article + **mujer**: feminine singular noun

the women

las: feminine plural article + **mujeres**: feminine plural noun

! *Hint: Always use a reliable reference source when you are not sure if a noun is masculine or feminine.*

Dictionaries and language textbooks indicate the gender of each Spanish noun, generally using **m.** for masculine and **f.** for feminine nouns. The use of the article with a noun to indicate gender is also common, for example, **el sombrero** or **la hamburguesa**.

We have presented articles and nouns together because articles provide so much information about nouns. However, articles can also be classified as adjectives. You will learn more about articles in Chapter 2, Adjectives.

PART TWO: USES OF SPANISH NOUNS
What Jobs Can Nouns Do?

1.6 Nouns as Subjects

Part Two takes a closer look at the jobs nouns can do. We build on what has been learned in Part One and use nouns together with other words to make sentences. You have learned to recognize the importance of gender and number of nouns. Use these skills when building sentences.

> **Nouns can perform many different jobs.**
> **By connecting nouns to other words,**
> **you are giving nouns a job to do.**

Consider the following English examples to make sure that you have a good understanding of subjects and objects. Spanish examples will follow later in the chapter, once you have a strong foundation in these concepts.

The pool is open.
|
Subject Noun

I love *the pool.*
|
Object Noun

Pool in both sentences is a noun. However, once a noun is placed within a sentence, different grammar terms differentiate between the various jobs nouns can do. In the sentence *The pool is open, pool* is used as a *subject.* In the second example, *I love the pool,* the noun *pool* is used as an *object.*

When you put a sentence together that is grammatically correct, you have given each part the right job to do.

The most important job nouns can do in a sentence is to act as a subject.

A sentence must have both a subject and a verb, and it must express a complete thought.

Look at the following examples.

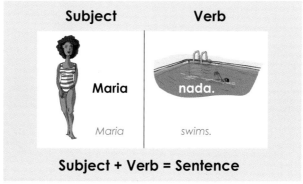

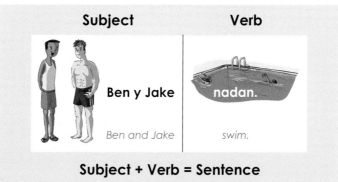

Beginners start by forming basic sentences that contain a subject and a verb. Names for people are nouns, too, and they are often the subject in a sentence. In both of the examples above, the person's name represents the subject. The verb form **nada** connects to the singular subject **Maria**, and the verb form **nadan** to the plural subject, **Ben y Jake**.

The *subject* of a sentence names the person(s) or thing(s) about which a statement is being made.

18

Each subject represents a building block. It connects to the verb in order to form a basic sentence. In both examples on the previous page, the subjects are people. In the following example, the subject is an inanimate object. Remember: Subjects can be either persons or things.

Los zapatos son grandes.

Subject of
the sentence

Verb

The shoes are big.

In this example, **los zapatos** (*the shoes*) is the subject of the sentence.

In all of these examples, the subject and the verb are the two main components that form the basic sentence.

A noun often does not stand alone with just a verb. A noun can be part of a group of words, with a main noun always at the heart of the group. Consider this group as a building block. Learn how to recognize the main noun in a group of words.

Here are some examples. We have placed a heart ♥ above the main Spanish noun. Look at the English equivalents for the Spanish groups of words. Some of them also consist of more than one word.

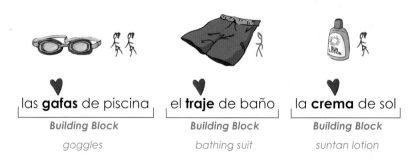

♥	♥	♥
las **gafas** de piscina	el **traje** de baño	la **crema** de sol
Building Block	**Building Block**	**Building Block**
goggles	bathing suit	suntan lotion

As the examples show, the nouns **gafas**, **traje**, and **crema** are the main nouns within each group. Each group of words serves as the subject. The article **las** indicates a feminine plural noun, **el** a masculine singular noun, and **la** a feminine singular noun.

Hint: Identify the number and gender of the subject noun before you place nouns in a sentence. Develop good habits: They help you avoid mistakes!

Jake es americano.   **Los zapatos** son grandes.

Simple Subject	Simple Subject
Jake is American.	*The shoes are big.*

In the sentence **Jake es americano**, **Jake** performs the action. **Jake**, a singular noun, is the subject of the sentence. When just one noun is used as the subject, it is called a *simple subject*.

In the second example, **los zapatos** (*the shoes*) is also a simple subject. This time, the one noun used as the simple subject is a plural noun.

> **A sentence has a *simple subject* if there is only one noun used as a subject, whether that subject is represented by a singular noun or a plural noun.**

A sentence may have two or more nouns used as subjects. In the examples below, the following four nouns are all used as subjects: **Ben**, **Jake**, **las pelotas**, and **el sombrero**.

Compound Subject   *Compound Subject*

Ben y Jake nadan.   **Las pelotas y el sombrero** están encima del armario.

Ben and Jake swim.   *The balls and the hat are on top of the locker.*

However, when two or more nouns used as subjects are joined by **y** (*and*), they form a *compound subject*. In the first example, two names—**Ben** and **Jake**—combine to form a compound subject. In the second example, a singular noun and a plural noun used as subjects—**las pelotas** and **el sombrero**—combine to form a compound subject. The term *compound subject* indicates that there is more than one noun used as a subject.

> **A sentence has a *compound subject* if there are two or more nouns used as subjects.**

! *Hint: A sentence can have a simple subject or a compound subject.*

1.7 Nouns Showing Possession

Nouns can show possession—relationship or ownership. This is an important concept, because a noun showing ownership or relationship often begins a sentence. In English, a noun with an apostrophe establishes a relationship between two nouns, such as between *sister* and *friend* in the first example below, and between *Susan* and *bathing suit* in the second.

Short English Version:

The following two examples show a different way that a noun can show possession in English. In this long English version, there is no apostrophe and the owner is introduced by the word "of." *My sister's friend* becomes *the friend of my sister,* and *Susan's bathing suit* becomes *the bathing suit of Susan.*

Long English Version:

 **The friend of my sister** is Mexican.

 **The bathing suit of Susan** is red.

> **The Spanish language does not use an apostrophe to show possession.**

The long English version can be used as a pattern when forming Spanish nouns showing possession.

Short English Version		Long English Version
my sister's friend	=	the friend of my sister
Susan's bathing suit	=	the bathing suit of Susan

The apostrophe is no longer needed, but the concept of ownership or relationship remains.

> **Two basic components are necessary when expressing possession—something that is being owned and an owner.**

Nouns Showing Possession

Long English Version	*Spanish*

the towel **of** Maria

the flippers **of** the boys

la toalla de Maria

las aletas de buceo de los chicos

> **The possession itself—the person, place, or thing that is owned—is placed before *de* and the owner.**

In the following example, the noun showing possession expresses a relationship. It also serves as the subject of the sentence.

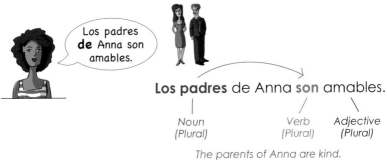

Los padres **de** Anna son amables.

Los padres de Anna **son** amables.

Noun (Plural)   Verb (Plural)   Adjective (Plural)

The parents of Anna are kind.

**A noun showing possession
can serve as a subject when forming sentences.**

When expressing relationships, pay attention to each noun before the **de**. In the example **Los padres de Anna**, the noun **los padres** is placed before **de Anna**. It is therefore the noun **los padres** that connects to the verb. **Los padres** is a plural noun and requires the plural verb form **son**. The adjective **amables** is also plural in form.

For now, we are showing you how to combine adjectives with nouns and what kinds of verbs are combined with nouns. Soon you will be making such choices yourself.

! *Hint: You might be surprised to realize how much you have already learned by starting your awareness early—it is a great way to sharpen basic skills!*

1.8 When Verbs Expand to Include Objects: Direct Objects

Let's turn our attention to another important concept: objects. Objects, like subjects, are nouns, but they have a different job to do in a sentence. Here is an example of a noun as subject:

The pool opens.
Subject Noun   Verb

Contrast the example above with the example below that uses the same noun, *pool*.

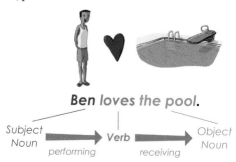

Ben loves the pool.
Subject Noun — performing → Verb — receiving → Object Noun

23

The basic unit of a sentence contains a subject and a verb. So far, our subjects are nouns. In the first example, *the pool* is the subject. The subject tells you what the sentence is all about, or who carries out the action.

In the second example, *the pool* is no longer the subject. Who carries out the action? *Ben* carries out the action, so the new subject is *Ben*. The sentence could end after the verb. However, it was expanded to include the noun *pool: Ben loves the pool. The pool* now receives the action of the verb *loves*.

When you are able to distinguish between a noun used as a subject and a noun used as an object, you recognize the relationships of nouns to other parts of the sentence.

The job each noun has to do is determined by the use of that noun in the sentence. In grammar, this is called *context*.

In this section, we are using nouns as direct objects.

The *direct object* is a word or group of words that directly receives the action expressed by the verb.

In grammar, the person or thing performing the action of the verb is called the *subject*. The person or thing receiving the action is called the *direct object*.

Subject ➡ Verb ➡ Direct Object

Think about what is needed to make this happen. Put the verb at center stage, because it is the verb that expresses the action that takes place. Only certain verbs allow you to add an object; they are action verbs. Not all verbs have the ability to include an object.

Use the graphic illustrations to guide you as you learn about nouns used as objects: The heart represents the verb *to love* (**amar**) and the hamburger represents the verb *to eat* (**comer**).

to love ♥   to eat 🍔

Verbs will be explained in detail in Chapter 4, but for this section, we selected the following two verbs: *to love* and *to eat*. Both verbs are now illustrated in examples with direct objects.

Direct Objects

People

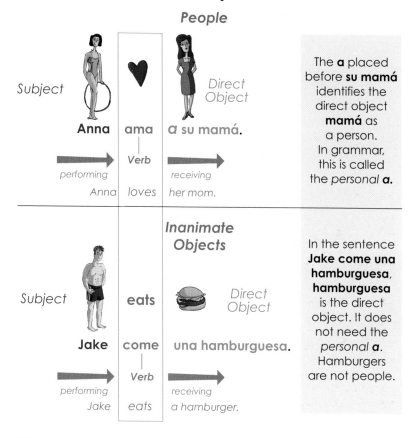

Subject		Direct Object	
Anna	ama	a su mamá.	The **a** placed before **su mamá** identifies the direct object **mamá** as a person. In grammar, this is called the *personal **a**.*
performing	Verb	receiving	
Anna	loves	her mom.	

Inanimate Objects

Subject		Direct Object	
Jake	eats come	una hamburguesa.	In the sentence **Jake come una hamburguesa**, **hamburguesa** is the direct object. It does not need the *personal **a**.* Hamburgers are not people.
performing	Verb	receiving	
Jake	eats	a hamburger.	

Notice the difference?

What is the reason to state two different categories for objects? The use of objects in the Spanish language requires you to make a distinction between people and inanimate objects, or things. For that reason, we selected the verb *to eat* and the verb *to love*. Both verbs can take direct objects. The verb *to eat* relates to things. What you eat is the direct object. The verb *to love* relates mainly to people. Whom you love is the direct object.

> **The personal *a* is placed before a noun used as a direct object if the object is a person or persons. The word *a* cannot be translated.**

❗ *Hint: Remember that **personal** a indicates "a person" to help you apply this rule correctly.*

The examples that follow give more details about subjects and objects.

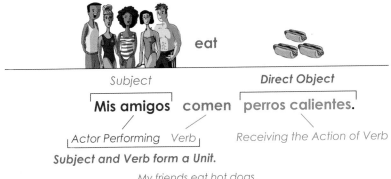

	eat	
Subject		Direct Object
Mis amigos comen		perros calientes.

Actor Performing · Verb · Receiving the Action of Verb

Subject and Verb form a Unit.

My friends eat hot dogs.

In the example above, two nouns are used. The job of the first noun, **mis amigos**, is to be the subject. Each subject must be followed by a verb. **Mis amigos** carries out the action of the verb *to eat*. **Mis amigos** is a plural noun, so the verb is **comen**. The sentence could end here, but it is extended to include a direct object. The second noun, **perros calientes**, is the direct object. Since it is an inanimate object, no personal ***a*** is needed.

| Subject | | Direct Object |
| **Mis amigos** aman | | a Maria. |

Actor Performing · Verb · Receiving the Action of Verb

Subject and Verb form a Unit.

My friends love Maria.

In this example, the plural noun **mis amigos** is still the subject. This time the verb *to love* is used. The verb is extended to include a direct object—a receiver. The receiving person is **Maria**. When talking about a person you love, you need to use the personal **a** in order to indicate that the object is a person. The direct object is **Maria**, placed after the **a**.

a · Maria

The use of pronouns, covered in detail in Chapter 3, will require you to know the type of nouns you are going to replace. Recognizing forms of nouns is therefore essential. With this knowledge in place, for example, you will find using object pronouns a lot easier. You will simply transfer the same concepts of gender and number of nouns to pronouns.

 If some of these concepts are beginning to make sense, you have made excellent progress. This chapter is not an easy one! Your progress indicates that you are building a solid foundation in Spanish.

You have learned about nouns being used as subjects and direct objects. Let us now introduce nouns as objects of prepositions.

1.9 Another Type of Object: Objects of Prepositions

There are two types of objects: direct objects and objects of prepositions. Direct objects receive the action of the verb directly. The other object works together with a preposition.

As the term *object of a preposition* indicates, a preposition combines with a noun used as an object; together they form a *prepositional phrase*. A *phrase* is made up of several words that are grouped together. In this book, phrases are considered to be building blocks.

A noun used after a preposition is called the *object of a preposition*.

Look at the words below; they are prepositions. We will cover this part of speech in more detail in Chapter 6. These examples serve only as a short introduction.

Examples of Spanish Prepositions

alrededor de	**encima de**	**a**

around	*on top of*	*to, into*

27

We also use the term *building block* for a prepositional phrase. Remember that building blocks need to be combined with other sentence parts in order to form a complete sentence.

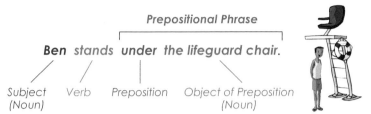

Prepositional Phrase

Ben *stands* **under** *the lifeguard chair.*

| Subject (Noun) | Verb | Preposition | Object of Preposition (Noun) |

In the English example above, the phrase *under the lifeguard chair* does not make sense standing alone. It must relate to another part of the sentence. In this case, the phrase relates to *Ben*.

As in English, nouns in Spanish are also used as objects of a preposition. However, two Spanish prepositions become part of a contraction when they are followed by a masculine singular noun. This has no parallel in English.

The following Spanish examples use a yellow contrast square to highlight these two contractions. Look at these examples carefully so you can recognize these contractions when you see them.

Objects of Prepositions

Preposition	+	Noun as Object of a Preposition	=	Prepositional Phrase

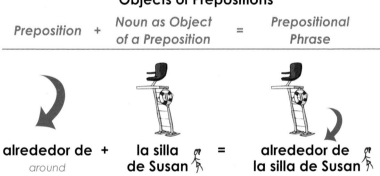

| **alrededor de** + | **la silla de Susan** | = | **alrededor de la silla de Susan** |
| *around* | *the lifeguard chair* | | *around the lifeguard chair* |

| **encima de** + | **el armario** | = | **encima del armario** |
| *on top of* | *the locker* | | *on top of the locker* |

Objects of Prepositions

Preposition	+	Noun as Object of a Preposition	=	Prepositional Phrase

a	+	**el vestuario**	=	**al vestuario**
into		*the locker room*		*into the locker room*

Spanish prepositions require you to carefully examine the noun that is used after the preposition. In Chapter 6, Prepositions, you will learn more about contractions in prepositional phrases. For now, these examples serve as an introduction, with more details to follow.

1.10 Details About Chapter Sequence

Because it is beneficial for the beginning language learner to take the lessons learned in one chapter and use them in the next, the chapter that follows is about adjectives. Throughout this chapter, many examples were illustrated using both nouns and adjectives so that you could see how closely they are linked. This gives you a head start on Chapter 2!

In addition, adjectives add words to the noun. When you use an adjective, you are often expanding the meaning of the subject. Because the subject is the heart of the sentence, it is very important to know how to identify and use it correctly. When you learn more about adjectives, you will strengthen these skills.

You are now ready to begin Chapter 2, Adjectives.

1.11 Overview of Spanish Nouns
Nouns That Name People

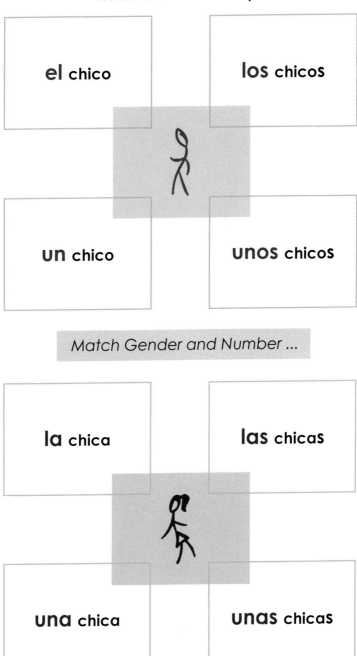

el chico

los chicos

un chico

unos chicos

Match Gender and Number ...

la chica

las chicas

una chica

unas chicas

Nouns That Name Inanimate Objects

el sombrero

los sombreros

un sombrero

unos sombreros

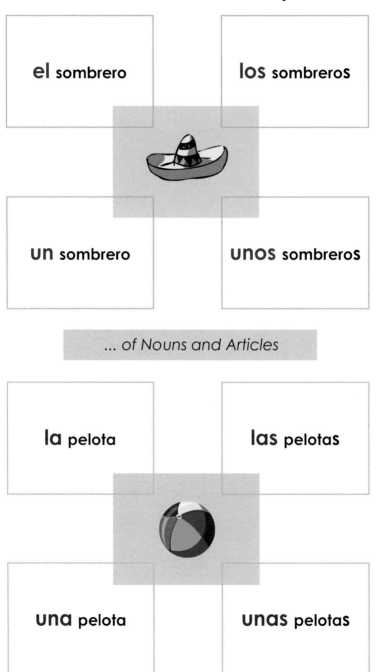

... of Nouns and Articles

la pelota

las pelotas

una pelota

unas pelotas

1.12 Spanish Noun Practice

Refer to the Spanish vocabulary words in the Introduction if you need help.

Practice One: Gender of Spanish Nouns

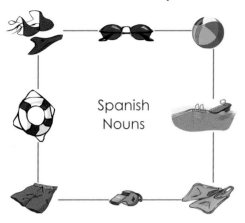

Write the total number of masculine nouns and the total number of feminine nouns in the appropriate box at the right.

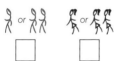

Practice Two: Number of Spanish Nouns

Write the total number of singular nouns and the total number of plural nouns (regardless of gender) in the appropriate box at the right.

CHAPTER 2

ADJECTIVES

2.1 Part One and Part Two Overview   34

PART ONE: FORM OF SPANISH ADJECTIVES
2.2 Descriptive Adjectives   35
2.3 Number and Gender of Descriptive Adjectives   37
2.4 Limiting Adjectives   40

PART TWO: USES OF SPANISH ADJECTIVES WITH NOUNS
2.5 Subjects: How to Form a Unit   59
2.6 A Practical Approach: When Adjectives Count   61
2.7 Details About Chapter Sequence   65
2.8 Overview of Spanish Adjectives   66
2.9 Spanish Adjective Practice   67

2.1 Part One and Part Two Overview

In this chapter, we look at how nouns expand to include adjectives in Spanish. In Part One, we introduce two groups of adjectives: *descriptive adjectives* and *limiting adjectives*. Here is a short overview:

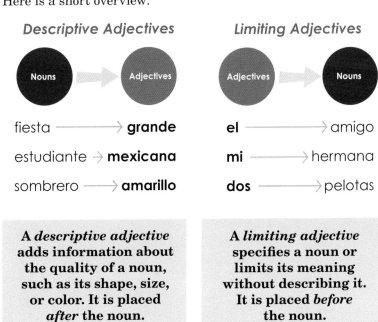

Descriptive Adjectives	Limiting Adjectives
fiesta ⟶ **grande**	**el** ⟶ amigo
estudiante ⟶ **mexicana**	**mi** ⟶ hermana
sombrero ⟶ **amarillo**	**dos** ⟶ pelotas

A *descriptive adjective* adds information about the quality of a noun, such as its shape, size, or color. It is placed *after* the noun.	A *limiting adjective* specifies a noun or limits its meaning without describing it. It is placed *before* the noun.

Nouns and adjectives go together. There are many rules to observe when adding adjectives to nouns.

In general, adjectives add more information about the noun. Once you are able to distinguish between the different kinds of adjectives, placement of Spanish adjectives becomes a lot easier.

In Part One, you will find details for each group, such as what kind of information adjectives can give. Part Two builds on what is covered in Part One, with the focus shifting from the form of adjectives to the use of adjectives. Soon you will be able to apply your knowledge about adjectives to form a sentence!

PART ONE: FORM OF SPANISH ADJECTIVES
What Information Do Adjectives Give?

2.2 Descriptive Adjectives

The information that adjectives express about nouns can take many forms.

> **An *adjective* is a word that describes a noun.**

Let's start with the first group: descriptive adjectives.

Descriptive adjectives primarily specify the shape, size, or color of a noun. To identify a descriptive adjective, ask the question "What kind?"

Descriptive adjectives are often called *common adjectives.* Like a common noun, they are ordinary, everyday adjectives. They describe nouns in a general way. Examples of English common adjectives include *soft, blue, sunny, small,* and *wet.*

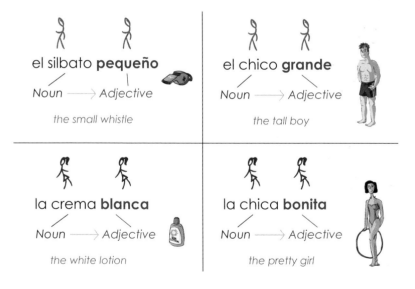

el silbato **pequeño**
Noun ⟶ Adjective
the small whistle

el chico **grande**
Noun ⟶ Adjective
the tall boy

la crema **blanca**
Noun ⟶ Adjective
the white lotion

la chica **bonita**
Noun ⟶ Adjective
the pretty girl

> **Descriptive adjectives add characteristics or features to a noun.**

Descriptive adjectives can be formed by using a proper noun. Adjectives based on nationalities are a form of descriptive adjective.

**In Spanish, descriptive adjectives
referring to nationalities are never capitalized.**

English Proper Noun	English Proper Adjective with Noun	Spanish Adjective with Noun
Mexico	**Mexican** student	estudiante **mexicana**
America	**American** hamburgers	hamburguesas **americanas**

Adjectives of nationality are covered again in Part Two.

Shortened Form of Some Adjectives

You have seen that descriptive adjectives in Spanish are placed *after* a noun. However, certain Spanish descriptive adjectives can be placed either *before* or *after* a noun. When they are placed before the noun they describe, they change form—a shortened form must be used.

You can see this in the following two examples.

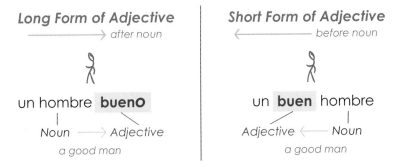

Long Form of Adjective
————→ after noun

un hombre **bueno**
Noun ——→ Adjective
a good man

Short Form of Adjective
←———— before noun

un **buen** hombre
Adjective ←—— Noun
a good man

In the first example, the complete form of the adjective **bueno** is used *after* the noun. In the second example, the adjective changes from **bueno** to **buen**, and this shortened form is now placed *before* the noun.

The noun used in each of the examples above is a masculine singular noun. This shortened form is used *only* before masculine singular nouns.

36

The same pattern can be used with **malo ~ mal** (*bad*).

The meaning of **bueno ~ buen** and **malo ~ mal** is the same whether the adjective is placed before or after the noun.

There are a few other adjectives that follow the same pattern. Remember the above examples well. We will use them again later on!

2.3 Number and Gender of Descriptive Adjectives

Many of the concepts you learned in Chapter 1 are applicable to Spanish adjectives.

Adjectives give information about number and gender through their form just like nouns do. Consider this section as an opportunity to review and strengthen your comprehension of the number and gender concepts.

Start with the noun and identify its *number*: Is it singular or plural? Next verify its *gender*: Is it masculine or feminine?

Spelling changes occur at the end of an adjective according to number and gender. To change the ending of the adjective, you must start with its masculine form.

> **The masculine form of an adjective determines the changes for the feminine form. Be prepared for consonant or vowel changes.**

Examine the next two charts closely. They will give you an overview of singular and plural adjective endings.

Singular Adjective Endings

Masculine Form of Adjective	Feminine Form of Adjective	Final Letters	Changes
Vowels			
grande	grande	♂ = **e** ♀ = **e**	Basic Rule: Adjectives ending in **-e** are unchanged when describing a feminine singular noun. *Examples:* **el colchón de aire grande, la pelota grande**
amarillo	amarilla	♂ = **o** ♀ = **a**	Basic Rule: Adjectives ending in **-o** change to **-a** when describing a feminine singular noun. *Examples:* **el sombrero amarillo, la toalla amarilla**
americano	americana	♂ = **o** ♀ = **a**	Some adjectives of nationality ending in **-o** change to **-a** when describing a feminine singular noun. *Examples:* **el chico americano, la chica americana**
Consonants			
inglés	inglesa	♂ = **s** ♀ = **s+a**	Basic Rule: Adjectives of nationality that end in a consonant add **-a** when describing a feminine singular noun. A written accent is not needed when the normal accent falls on the next to the last syllable. *Examples:* **el libro inglés, la escuela inglesa**

Plural Adjective Endings

Masculine Form of Adjective	Feminine Form of Adjective	Final Letters	Changes
 grandes	 **grandes**	♀ ♀ = **+S** ♂ ♂ = **+S**	Basic Rule: If the singular form of the adjective ends in a vowel, add -**s**. *Examples:* **los colchones grandes, las pelotas grandes**
 amarillos	 **amarillas**	♀ ♀ = **+S** ♂ ♂ = **+S**	*Examples:* **los sombreros amarillos, las toallas amarillas**
 americanos	 **americanas**	♀ ♀ = **+S** ♂ ♂ = **+S**	*Examples:* **los chicos americanos, las chicas americanas**
 ingleses	 **inglesas**	♀ ♀ = **+es** ♂ ♂ = **+S**	Basic Rule: For masculine forms: If the singular form of the adjective ends in a consonant, add -**es**. *Example:* **los libros ingleses** Basic Rule: For feminine forms: If the singular form of the adjective ends in a vowel, add -**s**. *Example:* **las escuelas inglesas**

Memorize masculine and feminine forms of adjectives. Because adjectives tell you about the gender and number of a noun through their form, if you can recognize the differences between these forms, you will also know whether the noun attached to the adjective is masculine or feminine.

2.4 Limiting Adjectives

The second group of Spanish adjectives is called *limiting adjectives*. This group includes the following: adjectives indicating quantity, articles, possessive adjectives, demonstrative adjectives, interrogative adjectives, and numerical adjectives. As the term indicates, limiting adjectives limit your choices. In contrast to descriptive adjectives placed *after* a noun, limiting adjectives are placed *before* a noun.

> ***Limiting adjectives* are placed before the noun.
> They tell you how many or which one.**

 mucho dinero

Adjectives Indicating Quantity

Words that indicate quantity are a common type of limiting adjective. They answer the question "How many?"

The following overview is based on the adjectives **mucho**, **poco**, and **todo**. It illustrates how the form of an adjective always corresponds to the noun it matches. Apply the concept of number as your first step. The singular form of an adjective is used with the singular form of a noun, and the plural form of an adjective with a plural noun. Apply the concept of gender next. Use the masculine form of an adjective with a masculine noun, and the feminine form with a feminine noun.

Number and Gender Concepts Combined

Number: One (Singular)   Number: More Than One (Plural)

Gender: Masculine or Feminine

 or   or

Adjectives Indicating Quantity

Meaning	Singular	Plural
a lot or much	mucho + masculine noun	muchos + masculine noun
	mucha + feminine noun	muchas + feminine noun
little or few	poco + masculine noun	pocos + masculine noun
	poca + feminine noun	pocas + feminine noun
all	todo + masculine noun	todos los + masculine noun
	toda + feminine noun	todas las + feminine noun

In the examples that follow, we will use these adjectives with nouns. **Todos**, a masculine plural adjective, needs a masculine plural noun, such as **chicos**. We use the same concepts when matching the feminine plural adjective **todas** with the noun **chicas**.

Todos los chicos nadan a las dos.

All the boys swim at 2 p.m.

Todas las chicas nadan a las tres.

All the girls swim at 3 p.m.

Above, we illustrate the use of the limiting adjectives **mucho** and **poco** with the noun **dinero**. Can you use your knowledge of number and gender to understand why the forms **mucho** and **poco** are used with **dinero**?

In the next example, **amigas** (feminine plural noun) takes the matching adjective form **muchas**.

> **Limiting adjectives can show quantity and are placed *before* the noun. They agree with their nouns in gender and number.**

Articles

Articles may also be labeled as adjectives. Articles introduce nouns. Therefore, they must be placed *before* the noun.

> ***Articles* specify whether a noun is referred to in a general or specific way.**

In this section, we are going to focus mainly on the indefinite articles **un**, **unos**, **una**, and **unas**. Just like the noun they

42

introduce, they show number and gender. All four articles refer to nouns in a general, rather than a specific, way.

The articles **un** before a masculine noun (**chico**) and **una** before a feminine noun (**chica**) are the equivalent of *a* or *an* in English. They are both *indefinite articles*.

The difference between the use of an indefinite and a definite article can best be understood by contrasting the two. Look at the following examples.

Indefinite Article: Un

Yo tengo **un** traje de baño. — General

Specific

El traje de baño está en el armario.

I have ***a*** bathing suit.

Definite Article: El

The bathing suit is in the locker.

When Jake talks about *a* bathing suit, **un traje de baño**, he is referring to the noun *bathing suit* in a general way.

For general statements, use an *indefinite article* before the noun. When being specific about a noun, use the *definite article*.

Contrast the first example, **Yo tengo un traje de baño** (*I have a bathing suit*), with **El traje de baño está en el armario** (*The bathing suit is in the locker*). Here, the use of **el** (*the*) indicates that you are referring to the noun *bathing suit* in a specific way. It is a particular bathing suit, not just any bathing suit.

The articles **unos** and **unas** are the plural forms of the indefinite article. They do not have an exact English equivalent, but are often translated as "some" or "a few."

Articles **are the most commonly used adjectives that introduce a noun. They agree in gender and number with the noun.**

Let's look at some examples using the plural indefinite article.

*I have **some** friends.*   mixed = masculine = **unos**

Some friends, in this case **unos amigos**, indicates that Ben is talking about a general group of friends. He is not specific about how many friends there are, or whether the group includes all males or both males and females.

However, by selecting the form **unos amigos**, Ben indicates that the group of friends includes at least one male. The number of males included in the group is not important. Even if only one male is present in a group, you must refer to that mixed group as masculine. (Not very fair, is it?)

> **The gender of a mixed group is determined by whether it includes at least one male. The masculine plural articles *unos* and *los* can indicate a combination of male and female persons or things.**

In the next example, definite articles are used to illustrate this concept with the noun **los padres**, referring to a group that includes a mother and a father.

the father   *the* mother   *the* parents

el padre   +   **la** madre   =   **los** padres

Remember the term limiting adjectives? Articles placed in front of a noun assist you in expressing these limits or differences when talking about people or inanimate objects.

! Hint: The concepts of number and gender should be familiar to you now. You will soon discover how they are used by pronouns.

Possessive Adjectives

Many possessive adjectives are based on subject pronouns. Let's begin with a chart of English subject pronouns.

English Subject Pronouns

			Masculine	Feminine	Neuter
Singular	① **I**	② **you**	③ **he**	**she**	*it*
Plural	① **we**	② **you**	③ **they**		

> **English possessive adjectives are based on subject pronouns. "He," "she," and "it" are the three English subject pronouns showing gender.**

English subject pronouns show gender only in the third-person singular: *he, she,* and *it.*

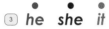

③ *he* **she** *it*

Remember that the third-person singular has *three* different subject pronouns: the "three in three" rule. This rule applies to both subject pronouns and possessive adjectives. You'll find this rule illustrated in the English possessive adjective chart below.

❗ Hint: Keep the details of these concepts in mind as you transfer some of this knowledge to the Spanish language.

Number Concept: The division between singular and plural is the red line on the English Possessive Adjectives chart below.

One   More than One

Gender Concept: The possessive adjectives *his, her,* and *its* are highlighted in the chart below.

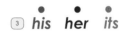

③ *his* **her** *its*

I, you, he, she, it, we, you, and *they* are called *personal pronouns.* In the term personal pronoun, the word "personal" relates to persons. Possessive adjectives, as the following chart illustrates, are derived from these personal pronouns. With the exception of *it,* all of them can relate to people, and all express the idea of showing possession.

English Possessive Adjectives

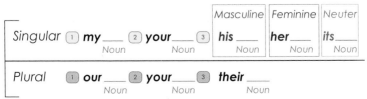

			Masculine	Feminine	Neuter
Singular	① **my** ___ Noun	② **your** ___ Noun	③ **his** ___ Noun	**her** ___ Noun	**its** ___ Noun
Plural	① **our** ___ Noun	② **your** ___ Noun	③ **their** ___ Noun		

45

Refer to the highlighted section of the chart: *his, her,* and *its*—
the three English possessive adjectives that show gender.
The "three in three" rule applies here. We will present more
details later.

Let's continue with two more English examples.

Anna is **my** sister.

Possessive Adjective · Noun

Lakewood is **our** pool.

Possessive Adjective · Noun

In the examples above, *my* and *our* are possessive adjectives.
They are placed before the noun.

How do limiting adjectives express ownership or relationship?

Limiting adjectives may be possessive adjectives. What do they
tell about the noun? It is *my* sister, not *your* sister. *My* before
sister shows relationship. *Our* pool states not *the* pool, but *our*
pool. The possessive adjective *our* placed before the noun *pool*
shows ownership. *My* and *our* give additional information about
the nouns they modify.

As in English, Spanish possessive adjectives express basic
information about relationship, ownership, and the nouns they
modify. However, they do it in a slightly different way.

Step 1 One

To help you understand this concept, we are going to use two
English examples first. This is step one. Step two will explain
the Spanish concept of relationship.

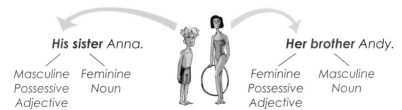

His sister Anna.

Masculine Feminine
Possessive Noun
Adjective

Her brother Andy.

Feminine Masculine
Possessive Noun
Adjective

Masculine Possessive Adjective
+ Feminine Noun

Feminine Possessive Adjective
+ Masculine Noun

46

The possessive adjective expresses *ownership* or *relationship*. In English, the possessive adjectives *his* and *her* refer to the person who possesses or relates to something or someone.

In the first example, *his* modifies the noun *sister*. In the second example, *her* modifies the noun *brother*.

If you take a closer look, you will see that *Andy,* the owner, labels the feminine noun *Anna* as his sister. In the second example, *Anna,* the owner, labels a masculine noun, *Andy,* as her brother.

English possessive adjectives relate to the *owner*.

Step Two

Let's take a close look at the example **Lakewood es nuestra piscina** (*Lakewood is our pool*).

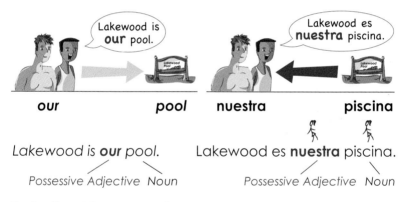

In the Spanish sentence, the possessive adjective must match the noun **la piscina** in number and gender. Once you have determined that **la piscina** is a feminine singular noun, you must select a possessive adjective that is also feminine and singular in form. **Nuestra** (*our*) is the correct choice.

**Spanish possessive adjectives match
the *noun that is possessed*—not the owner!**

Hint: Just as you learned in the articles section, Spanish possessive adjectives show number and gender through their form. Transfer this basic concept to Spanish possessive adjectives. It will make your job a lot easier.

You have already learned to use what we call the matching game for descriptive adjectives and articles. You are now well prepared to learn more about Spanish possessive adjectives.

Overview: Spanish Possessive Adjectives

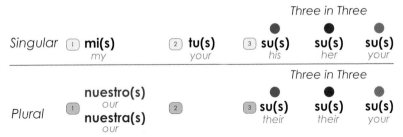

Note: The Spanish second-person plural form is not included in the chart. That form is used mainly in Spain and is not covered in this book.

> **In Spanish, each possessive adjective has both a singular and a plural form.**

Take a closer look at **nuestro** and **nuestra**. What information can these two forms give you? This possessive adjective has two separate forms: **Nuestro** is used with a masculine noun, and **nuestra** is used with a feminine noun.

> **Only the possessive adjectives *nuestro* and *nuestra* show gender through their form.**

Mi and **tu** are the singular forms of *my* and *your*. **Mis** (*my*) and **tus** (*your*) are the plural forms. Refer to the illustrations below to see how they are used with nouns.

Spanish Possessive Adjectives *Mi(s)* and *Tu(s)* Singular and Plural

There are three English subject pronouns that show gender: *he, she,* and *it.* Likewise, three English possessive adjectives show gender: *his, her,* and *its.* You must remember that the English subject pronoun *it* has no Spanish equivalent and, therefore, there is also no Spanish equivalent for the possessive adjective *its. Its* must be thought of as *his* or *her* in Spanish.

Mi and **tu** in the singular and **mis** and **tus** in the plural follow the same pattern as **su** and **sus,** as illustrated in the charts below.

> **The possessive adjectives *su* and *sus* serve a double function: Depending on the noun they modify, these adjectives can indicate either singular or plural. They can both be translated as "his," "her," "your," or "their."**

"Three in Three"

Subject Pronoun	**él** ●	**ella** ●	**usted** ●
Singular Possessive Adjective **Su**	(3) **su** _Noun_ *his*	**su** _Noun_ *her*	**su** _Noun_ *your*
Plural Possessive Adjective **Sus**	(3) **sus** _Nouns_ *his*	**sus** _Nouns_ *her*	**sus** _Nouns_ *your*

Subject Pronoun	**ellos** ●	**ellas** ●	**ustedes** ●
Singular Possessive Adjective **Su**	(3) **su** _Noun_ *their*	**su** _Noun_ *their*	**su** _Noun_ *your*
Plural Possessive Adjective **Sus**	(3) **sus** _Nouns_ *their*	**sus** _Nouns_ *their*	**sus** _Nouns_ *your*

We conclude our brief introduction to Spanish possessive adjectives by presenting the same information in several charts with specific examples.

Possessive Adjective **Su**: *His, Her, Your*
Possessive Adjective **Sus**: *His, Her, Your*
Possessive Adjectives **Nuestro(s)** and **Nuestra(s)**: *Our*
Possessive Adjectives **Su** and **Sus**: *Their*

Possessive Adjective *Su*: His, Her, Your

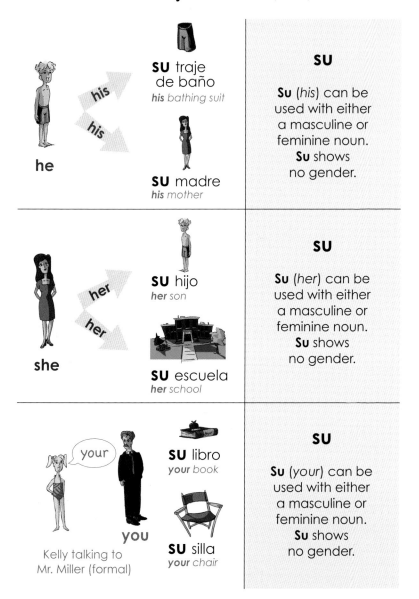

SU traje de baño
his bathing suit

SU madre
his mother

he

SU

Su (*his*) can be used with either a masculine or feminine noun. **Su** shows no gender.

SU hijo
her son

SU escuela
her school

she

SU

Su (*her*) can be used with either a masculine or feminine noun. **Su** shows no gender.

your

you

Kelly talking to Mr. Miller (formal)

SU libro
your book

SU silla
your chair

SU

Su (*your*) can be used with either a masculine or feminine noun. **Su** shows no gender.

Su can mean *his, her,* or *your.*

The possessive adjective **su**, meaning *your,* will be easier to understand after you have learned more about the pronoun "you" in Chapter 3, Pronouns.

Possessive Adjective *Sus*: His, Her, Your

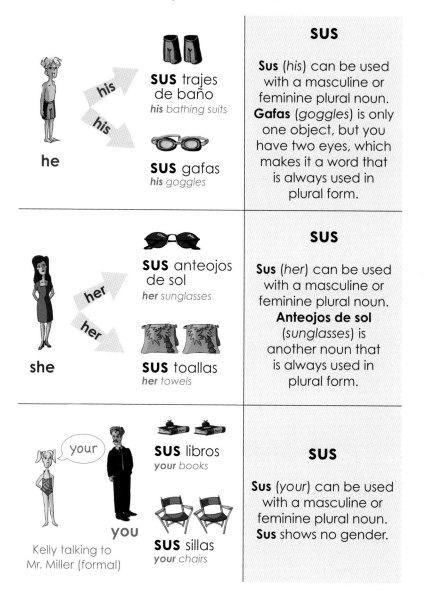

SUS trajes
de baño
his bathing suits

SUS gafas
his goggles

he

SUS

Sus (*his*) can be used
with a masculine or
feminine plural noun.
Gafas (*goggles*) is only
one object, but you
have two eyes, which
makes it a word that
is always used in
plural form.

SUS anteojos
de sol
her sunglasses

SUS toallas
her towels

she

SUS

Sus (*her*) can be used
with a masculine or
feminine plural noun.
Anteojos de sol
(*sunglasses*) is
another noun that
is always used in
plural form.

SUS libros
your books

you

Kelly talking to
Mr. Miller (formal)

SUS sillas
your chairs

SUS

Sus (*your*) can be used
with a masculine or
feminine plural noun.
Sus shows no gender.

Sus can mean *his, her,* or *your.*

Mi(s), **tu(s)**, and **su(s)** show no gender in form. However, the
plural possessive adjective we will examine next is different.
The Spanish adjective for *our* shows gender in form. There
is a masculine form, **nuestro**, and a feminine form, **nuestra**.
Specific examples follow.

51

Possessive Adjectives *Nuestro(s)* and *Nuestra(s)*: Our

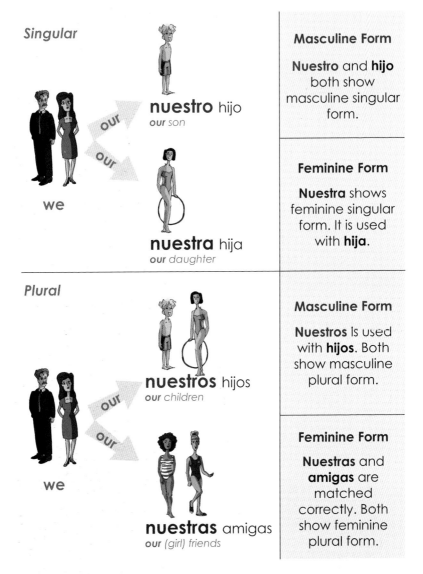

Singular	**nuestro** hijo *our son*	**Masculine Form** **Nuestro** and **hijo** both show masculine singular form.
we	**nuestra** hija *our daughter*	**Feminine Form** **Nuestra** shows feminine singular form. It is used with **hija**.
Plural	**nuestros** hijos *our children*	**Masculine Form** **Nuestros** Is used with **hijos**. Both show masculine plural form.
we	**nuestras** amigas *our (girl) friends*	**Feminine Form** **Nuestras** and **amigas** are matched correctly. Both show feminine plural form.

You can use every possessive adjective except **nuestro(s)** and **nuestra(s)** without paying attention to the gender of the nouns they are modifying.

! *Hint: When using* **mis**, **tus**, **sus**, **nuestros**, *and* **nuestras**, *be sure to add a plural noun.*

Possessive Adjectives *Su* and *Sus*: Their

	Singular	**SU**
they	**SU** perro *their dog*	**Su** can be used with a masculine or feminine singular noun.
	Plural	**SUS**
	SUS toallas *their bathing suits*	**Sus** can be used with a masculine or feminine plural noun.

	Singular	**SU**
they	**SU** piscina *their pool*	**Su** can be used with a masculine or feminine singular noun.
	Plural	**SUS**
	SUS anteojos de sol *their sunglasses*	**Sus** can be used with a masculine or feminine plural noun.

	Singular	**SU**
you Kelly talking to Mr. and Mrs. Miller (formal)	**SU** escuela *your school*	**Su** can be used with a masculine or feminine singular noun.
	Plural	**SUS**
	SUS libros *your books*	**Sus** can be used with a masculine or feminine plural noun.

The many different meanings of **su** and **sus** can only be learned as you use them in context.

Possessive adjectives before nouns express relationship or ownership. You can also express relationship or ownership by using **de** (*of*) between two nouns.

The following examples illustrate these two ways to express ownership. **El libro de Charles** (*the book of Charles*) uses the **de** (*of*) pattern. **Su libro** (*his book*) illustrates relationship by using the possessive adjective with the noun. **El libro de Charles** and **su libro** both express *Charles'* ownership of *the book*.

Possession
(What is being owned?)

Owner
(Who is the owner?)

el libro **de** Charles

SU libro

You must avoid trying to use the English pattern with an apostrophe (*Charles' book*) in Spanish. There is no apostrophe in Spanish.

la silla **de** Susan

SU silla

los amigos **de** Maria

SUS amigos

las toallas **de** Ben

SUS toallas

You will learn more about the use of **su** as you progress.

Demonstrative Adjectives

Demonstrative adjectives point out persons or things. Is the person or thing discussed near or far? The relationship in terms of distance is often important.

> **Spanish *demonstrative adjectives*
> point out persons or things.**

54

Let's introduce English examples first to give you a better understanding of the Spanish demonstrative adjectives. There is one important parallel between English and Spanish demonstrative adjectives: Both show the number of the noun they modify. *This* and *that* are singular adjectives; *these* and *those* are plural adjectives.

Consider the following example. It illustrates the difference between *this* and *that* in terms of the distance between the speaker and what is being discussed.

Singular: Refers to one person or thing

| esta **hamburguesa** | esa **hamburguesa** |
| *this* hamburger | *that* hamburger |

Both English and Spanish adjectives show number. Spanish adjectives also include the concept of gender.

Distance

This as **este** (masculine singular) or **esta** (feminine singular) and *these* as **estos** (masculine plural) or **estas** (feminine plural) indicate persons, places, or things *close to the speaker*. Note that the noun modified provides a clue to the required form.

Demonstrative Adjectives

Gender	Number	Adjective	Noun
Masculine	Singular	est**e**	chic**o**
	Plural	est**os**	chic**os**
Feminine	Singular	est**a**	chic**a**
	Plural	est**as**	chic**as**

A Spanish demonstrative adjective shows the number and gender of the noun it modifies.

That as **ese** (masculine singular) or **esa** (feminine singular) and *those* as **esos** (masculine plural) or **esas** (feminine plural) refer to persons, places, or things *at a distance from the speaker*. Again, note that the noun modified gives a clue to the required form.

Demonstrative Adjectives

Gender	Number	Adjective	Noun
Masculine	Singular	es**e**	chic**o**
	Plural	es**os**	chic**os**
Feminine	Singular	es**a**	chic**a**
	Plural	es**as**	chic**as**

Demonstrative adjectives have no accent.

In Chapter 3, Pronouns, we compare and contrast demonstrative adjectives and demonstrative pronouns. Placed side by side, both are easier to understand.

! *Hint: Demonstrative adjectives do not have accents and must be followed by a noun. However, the same word **with** an accent is a demonstrative pronoun, and it stands alone.*

In the next section, you will see many parallels between interrogative and demonstrative adjectives.

Interrogative Adjectives

Interrogative adjectives add the concept of asking a question to the noun. The term *interrogative* also exists in Spanish. In Spanish, a question word is called **una palabra interrogativa.** As a limiting adjective, it is placed *before* the noun it modifies.

An *interrogative adjective* is used to form a question. Just like other limiting adjectives, it is used *before* the noun it modifies.

Observe the accents, and note the additional punctuation when beginning a question.

¿**Qué hora** es?

Question Word Noun   *What time is it? (Literally, What hour is it?)*

Qué is the interrogative adjective that modifies the noun **hora.** By adding the word **qué**, you are able to form a question. Note that **qué** does not show number or gender.

The examples that follow use the question words **cuánto(s)** and **cuánta(s).** Both translate as *how much* or *how many* in English.

56

Note the *singular* and *plural* as well as the *masculine* and *feminine* forms of these adjectives.

¿**Cuántos años** tienes?

/ \
Question Word   Noun

How old are you?
(Literally, How many years do you have?)

The question words **cuánto(s)** and **cuánta(s)** show both number and gender. In the example above, the question word **cuántos** matches the noun **años** in indicating masculine plural form.

Here are two more examples.

Cuántos is used with the masculine plural noun **chicos**, and **cuántas** is used with the feminine plural noun **chicas**.

> **Most question words must match the number and gender of the noun that follows.**

When limiting adjectives were first introduced, you learned about adjectives indicating quantity. Now you will see how specific numbers can be used as adjectives to show quantity.

Numerical Adjectives

Numerical adjectives refer to quantity by using specific numbers in an adjective-noun combination. Study the summary of cardinal and ordinal numbers that follows.

Cardinal number = **c** for **c**ounting: 1, 2, 3 or one, two, three.

1	**2**	**3**	**4**	5	**6**	**7**	8	9	**10**
uno	dos	tres	cuatro	cinco	seis	siete	ocho	nueve	diez

Ordinal number = **o** for **o**rdered sequence: 1st, 2nd, 3rd or first, second, third.

! *Hint: When counting, start with* **un0**, *then* **dos**, **tres**, *etc.*

Numerical adjectives are based on cardinal numbers.
The following examples show numerical adjectives before
a masculine noun.

un perro caliente	**dos** perros calientes	**tres** perros calientes
one/a hot dog	*two hot dogs*	*three hot dogs*

> **When the numerical adjective expressing "one"**
> **precedes a masculine noun, its form is *un*, not *uno*.**

As shown in the example above, **un perro caliente** can be
translated as either *one hot dog* (**un** = numerical adjective)
or *a hot dog* (**un** = indefinite article). If the noun is feminine,
the pattern is the same: **una pelota** can be translated as either
one ball (**una** = numerical adjective) or *a ball* (**una** = indefinite
article). A numerical adjective expressing the concept of the
number *one* matches the noun that follows in gender as well
as number.

11	**12**	**13**	**14**	15
once	doce	trece	catorce	quince

16	**17**	**18**	**19**	20
dieciséis	diecisiete	dieciocho	diecinueve	veinte

¿Cuántos años tienes?

Tengo **dieciséis** años.

16 dieciséis

Tengo **dieciséis años**.

Numerical Adjective (Plural) Noun (Plural)

I am sixteen years old.
(Literally, I have sixteen years.)

The numerical adjective **dieciséis** (*sixteen*) refers to more than one. Therefore, the noun that follows must be plural: **años**.

! *Hint: Remember that a noun that follows a numerical adjective must match it in number. Use the plural form of a noun after any number indicating more than one.*

Numbers used as adjectives modify a noun. The noun that follows the number shows singular or plural form depending on the number used.

This concludes Part One. In Part Two, we will explain how nouns and adjectives serve as subjects in sentences.

PART TWO:
USES OF SPANISH ADJECTIVES WITH NOUNS
What Jobs Do Adjectives Do?

2.5 Subjects: How to Form a Unit

Simple sentences, or units, are composed of a subject and a verb. Beginners in Spanish often form sentences that start out as noun-adjective combinations. You can create a basic sentence from a noun-adjective combination by inserting the verb *to be* between the noun and the adjective. In both English and Spanish, the adjective following the linking verb *to be* adds details about the subject.

The examples below show noun-adjective combinations, which represent *building blocks*.

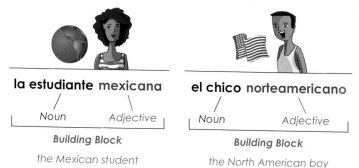

la estudiante mexicana	**el chico** norteamericano
Noun — Adjective	Noun — Adjective
Building Block	*Building Block*
the Mexican student	*the North American boy*

The number and gender of the adjective must match the number and gender of the noun. **La estudiante**, a feminine singular noun, requires an adjective that is also feminine singular: **mexicana**. The adjective **norteamericano** is masculine singular and is used with the masculine singular noun **chico**.

59

A noun standing alone or combined with an adjective represents only a building block, not a complete unit.

If you separate the descriptive adjective from the noun and place it after *to be,* you must be careful to keep the noun-adjective agreement. The noun and adjective must match in number and gender even when the adjective is separated from the noun.

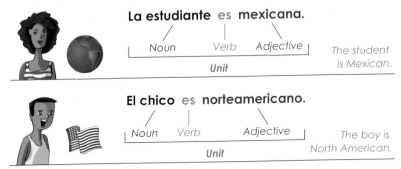

La estudiante es mexicana.

| Noun | Verb | Adjective |

Unit

The student is Mexican.

El chico es norteamericano.

| Noun | Verb | Adjective |

Unit

The boy is North American.

The examples above illustrate how you can create a short sentence by separating the descriptive adjective from the noun and placing it after a form of the verb *to be.* The nouns **estudiante** and **chico** remain, but they are now subjects of the basic sentences you have formed. The adjectives follow the verb **es** and are used as complements, giving details about the subjects. They still agree in number and gender with the noun. By using the pattern of noun-verb-adjective, you formed two basic sentences. Each sentence is a *unit.*

**Descriptive adjectives following the verb forms
es ("is") and *son* ("are") give details about the subject.**

The following examples all use a variation of **padres** (*parents*) as the subject.

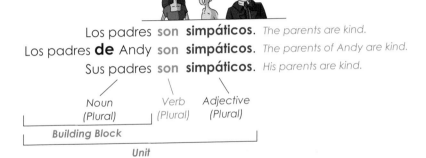

Los padres **son simpáticos.** *The parents are kind.*
Los padres **de** Andy **son simpáticos.** *The parents of Andy are kind.*
Sus padres **son simpáticos.** *His parents are kind.*

| Noun | Verb | Adjective |
| (Plural) | (Plural) | (Plural) |

| Building Block |

Unit

> **A noun showing possession, either as ownership or relationship, can serve as the subject when forming sentences.**

The most important noun in **los padres de Andy** is **los padres**. This noun connects to the verb **son**. **Los padres** is the subject in this group of words. In form, **los padres** is plural. When using a plural noun, you must use a verb form that is also plural. The verb form has been added for you in this sentence. In Chapter 4, Verbs, you will learn how to connect nouns to verbs.

The next section will steer away from dry grammar. Its focus is on a more practical use of adjectives.

2.6 A Practical Approach: When Adjectives Count

This section emphasizes the importance of understanding idiomatic expressions and how they relate to the use of adjectives. It will give you a deeper understanding of the role adjectives play when used in context for the purpose of communication.

Language
is
Communication

Every language uses phrases or expressions that are difficult for a non-native speaker to understand. The illustrations below show examples of two English expressions that a Spanish-speaking person would not necessarily understand.

You're driving me up the wall!   *Someone kicked the bucket.*

To help you understand this type of idiomatic expression, read the following three definitions of idioms.

1. A phrase or expression that means something different from what the words actually say. An idiom is usually understandable to a particular group of people.

2. An expression that cannot be immediately understood by analyzing its literal meaning.

3. A group of words that, taken as a whole, has a meaning different from that of the sum of the individual words.

 Spanish, like English, has many idiomatic expressions. Although their literal translations sound odd to English speakers, they sound perfectly natural to native speakers, just like "You're driving me up the wall!" sounds perfectly natural to an English speaker.

Let's analyze the example of expressing "you're welcome." In Spanish, one way to express this idea is the use of **de nada**. **Nada** basically means "nothing." **De nada** translates as "don't mention it" or "you're welcome" in English.

If you look up the word "welcome" in an English-Spanish dictionary and find the word **bienvenido**, you might think it means "you're welcome." However, that is not the case.

The following examples show how the term **bienvenido** *is* used.

The Miller family visits Maria in
═══Mexico!═══

Bienvenid**a**, Anna!

Welcome, Anna!

Bienvenid**o**, Andy!

Welcome, Andy!

Bienvenid**os**!

Welcome!

As the examples show, the adjective **bienvenido** is generally used as a welcoming greeting. If it is used to address a male (Andy) it takes the form **bienvenido**. Addressing Anna, a female, it is changed to **bienvenida**. For a group of mixed gender, use **bienvenidos** to show the plural. If you have a group of girls, use **bienvenidas**. The adjective must match the noun it refers to in both number and gender.

Anna, Andy, and their parents could each say "thank you" in response to Maria's warm welcome.

Much**as** gracias.
Thank you. / Many thanks.

Thank you could be one way of translating **muchas gracias**. Would you agree that the English translation of *many thanks* is a lot closer to the Spanish way of saying thanks? By using *many thanks,* you focus on the plural form of **gracias**. **Muchas** is the feminine plural form of the adjective **mucho** (*much*).

You could also express *It is a pleasure to meet you.* That idiomatic expression also uses **mucho**.

Mucho gusto.
It is a pleasure to meet you.
(Literally, *Much pleasure.*)

! *Hint: Can you tell by the form of* **mucho** *that the noun that follows will be masculine singular? If you can, you are well on your way to understanding how adjectives and nouns must match in number and gender.*

Depending on what time the Miller family arrives, each member could respond with the following general greetings that refer to the specific time of the day.

Buenos días.
Good morning.

Buenas tardes.
Good afternoon.

Buenas noches.
Good night.

Are you able to recognize the different adjective forms **buenos** and **buenas**? If you do, you understand that the masculine noun **día** requires the masculine form of the adjective **bueno**.

In Spanish, this greeting is used in the plural. **Buenos** matches **días**. The two other greetings are both based on feminine nouns: **la tarde** and **la noche**. For both, you must change the adjective to **buena**. *The afternoon* and *the night* must also be used in the plural. **Buenas tardes** and **buenas noches** are the correct matches.

In Spanish, there are a number of idiomatic expressions with the verb **hacer** (literal meaning, *to do* or *to make*) that are used to describe the weather.

¿Qué tiempo hace en los Estados Unidos?
What's the weather like in the United States?

Focus on two adjectives introduced in Part One of this chapter: **buen** and **mal**. Both are placed *before* the noun.

¿Hace **buen** tiempo?
*Is the weather **good**?*

No, hace **mal** tiempo.
*No, the weather is **bad**.*

When talking about the weather, you can use **mucho** to emphasize nouns like **calor** (*heat*) or **sol** (*sun*). As a contrast, you can use the adjective **poco** (*little*) to stress a lesser degree of quality for the nouns. We include common English translations for each example.

Hace **mucho** calor.
*It's **very** hot.*

Hace **mucho** sol.
*It's **very** sunny.*

Hace **poco** calor.
*It's **hardly** warm.*

Hace **poco** sol.
*It's **hardly** sunny.*

While the adjective **mucho** is usually translated as *much* or *a lot of,* and the adjective **poco** is usually translated as *little,* translating Spanish idioms is a challenge when you want to find appropriate words. A literal translation is possible, but it often makes no sense. You might find an English translation that better expresses the meaning for an English speaker. *It's very hot* and *It's very sunny* express the Spanish meaning clearly, as do *It's hardly warm* and *It's hardly sunny.* These sentences use the English adverbs *very* and *hardly* rather than the English adjectives *much* and *little,* which sound awkward.

We will end this chapter by explaining what to expect next. The sequence of chapters plays an important role in setting the stage for learning basic language skills.

2.7 Details About Chapter Sequence

We have now covered two important parts of speech: nouns and adjectives. You know that nouns are the names of persons, places, and things, and you know that adjectives are words that add meaning to nouns.

While you were learning about adjectives in this chapter, you had a chance to review what you already knew about nouns. Your next step will be to progress from nouns to pronouns. Pronouns take the place of nouns, and they build on what you have learned in Chapters 1 and 2.

Although the different kinds of pronouns will be new to you, the jobs that they do will be familiar. The form changes from noun to pronoun, but the function remains the same: Both nouns and pronouns are used as subjects and as objects within a sentence. Since you have already learned what kind of jobs nouns can do, it will be easy to transfer that knowledge to pronouns.

In this chapter, you became more familiar with the two concepts of number and gender in your study of adjectives. These concepts will be very important in your study of pronouns.

You are now ready to begin Chapter 3, Pronouns.

2.8 Overview of Spanish Adjectives

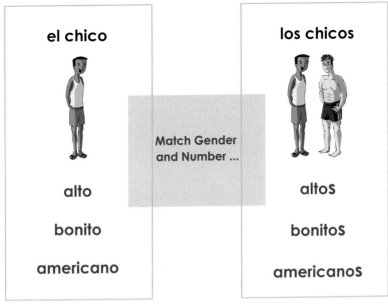

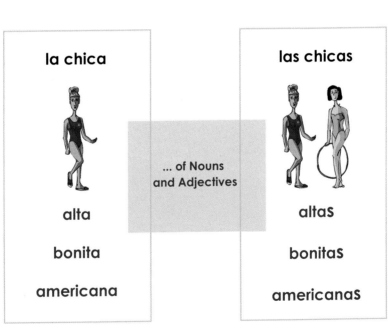

2.9 Spanish Adjective Practice

Refer to the Spanish vocabulary words in the Introduction if you need help.

Practice One: Indefinite Articles

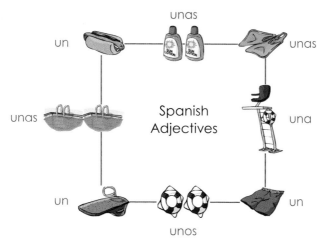

Write the total number of each type of indefinite article in the appropriate box at the right.

Practice Two: Descriptive and Limiting Adjectives

Write the total number of descriptive adjectives and the total number of limiting adjectives in the appropriate box at the right.

Descriptive Adjectives   Limiting Adjectives

CHAPTER 3

PRONOUNS

3.1 Part One and Part Two Overview 70

PART ONE: FORM OF SPANISH PRONOUNS

3.2 Introduction 70
3.3 Common Spanish Personal Pronouns 71
3.4 Grammar Person 74
3.5 Number of Spanish Personal Pronouns 78
3.6 Gender of Spanish Personal Pronouns 79
3.7 Pronouns Pointing Out People or Things 83
3.8 Pronouns Forming Questions 84

PART TWO: USES OF SPANISH PRONOUNS

3.9 Introduction: "You" Alert 87
3.10 Singular Pronouns: **Tú** and **Usted** 88
3.11 Plural Pronoun: **Ustedes** 90
3.12 A Great Start: Using Subject Pronouns 92
3.13 Overview of Subject and Direct Object Pronouns 93
3.14 Direct Object Pronouns 93
3.15 A Different Job: Object Pronouns with Prepositions 97
3.16 Details About Chapter Sequence 98
3.17 Spanish Pronoun Practice 99

Nouns Adjectives Pronouns Verbs Adverbs Prepositions Conjunctions Interjections

3.1 Part One and Part Two Overview

Part One takes a closer look at the different forms that pronouns can have. *Pronouns* do the same jobs that nouns do, but their forms are different.

My (girl)friend Maria is pretty.   She is pretty.

The personal pronouns covered in this chapter include subject pronouns and direct object pronouns. Other pronouns included here are object pronouns with prepositions, demonstrative pronouns, and interrogative pronouns.

Part Two includes sections that cover the different uses of the Spanish pronouns for English "you," where they are explained in the context of sentences.

Because pronouns are substitutes for nouns, many concepts already covered in Chapters 1 and 2 are repeated here. This review will help you to improve your understanding of some of the fundamental concepts of the Spanish language.

My friend Jake is tall.   He is tall.

A new concept covered in this chapter is the use of accents in words. We show you how accents can change the meaning of certain words.

PART ONE: FORM OF SPANISH PRONOUNS
What Information Do Pronouns Give?

3.2 Introduction

Pronouns: Substitutes For Nouns
Personal Pronouns

Masculine			Feminine		
Noun		*Pronoun*	*Noun*		*Pronoun*
el hombre		**él**	**la** madre		**ella**
el niño		**él**	**la** chica		**ella**
el chico		**él**	**la** estudiante		**ella**
el perro caliente		**él**	**la** crema		**ella**
el traje de baño		**él**	**la** silla		**ella**

A substitute teacher does the job of your regular teacher when the regular teacher is not there. A different person does the job, but the job is the same—teaching! Similarly, pronouns are substitutes for the nouns they replace. The chart above illustrates the shift from nouns to pronouns.

3.3 Common Spanish Personal Pronouns

The prefix "pro-" in the word *pronoun* means "for." The word *pronoun* simply means "for a noun" or "in place of a noun." Keep this definition in mind as we cover pronouns. Using pronouns can help you avoid monotonous repetition.

Before giving an overview of Spanish pronouns, we will
introduce the most common personal pronouns.

He/She/It/They
Personal Pronouns

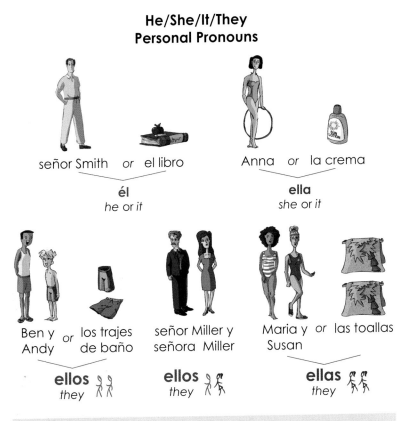

señor Smith *or* el libro

él
he or it

Anna *or* la crema

ella
she or it

Ben y Andy *or* los trajes de baño

ellos
they

señor Miller y señora Miller

ellos
they

Maria y Susan *or* las toallas

ellas
they

It is essential to learn the gender of each noun. Unless you have
identified the gender of a noun, you will not be able to select the
correct pronoun substitute for it.

Masculine singular nouns are replaced by the pronoun **él**.
The use of an accent changes the meaning of the word from
el (*the*)—the mascular singular definite article—to **él** (*he*),
which is used as a pronoun that stands alone.

Let's continue with a chart that illustrates forms and usage of the Spanish pronouns for English "we."

I/We
Personal Pronouns

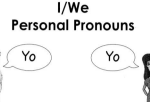

In Spanish, important changes happen when you make the shift from *I* to *we*. Refer to the charts that follow for more details.

In form, pronouns show number and gender just like nouns do.

> **Form** refers to the qualities and characteristics that pronouns have in common.

Grammar person is a new concept that you will learn with pronouns.

A short overview introduces number, gender, and grammar person. Following this short overview, each of these three qualities, which are found in most pronouns, is covered separately in greater detail.

Information Expressed by Pronouns

Number	Grammar Person

Number

Singular Pronoun
yo, tú, él, ella, usted
I, you, he, she, you

Plural Pronoun
nosotros, nosotras, ellos, ellas, ustedes
we, we, they, they, you

Grammar Person

1 Person speaking

2 Person spoken to

3 Person or thing spoken about

Gender

Andy *or* **él**
Masculine (Singular)

Maria *or* **ella**
Feminine (Singular)

nosotros **nosotros**
Masculine (Plural)

nosotras **nosotras**
Feminine (Plural)

Details about each group—number, gender, and grammar person—follow.

3.4 Grammar Person

In grammar, there is a system that is used to classify pronouns. It is called *grammar person*.

The relationship between pronouns and verbs is important when building sentences. Before using verbs correctly, you must be able to understand the categories of pronouns based on grammar person. In Chapter 4, Verbs, we explain how the pattern of the grammar person extends to the use of the different verb forms.

Start with the first big step: pronouns.

> **The basic pronouns used for communication are grouped into three categories: person(s) speaking, person(s) spoken to, and person(s) or thing(s) spoken about.**

Classification by grammar person divides pronouns into three groups, each of which includes both singular and plural pronouns. However, the contrast in color in the charts in this chapter distinguishes between singular and plural. Yellow symbols indicate *singular* pronouns, and orange symbols indicate *plural* pronouns.

Grammar Person

1	*Person speaking*	1	*Persons speaking*
2	*Person spoken to*	2	*Persons spoken to*
3	*Person or thing spoken about; Person spoken to (**you**, formal)*	3	*Persons or things spoken about; Persons spoken to (**you**, formal and informal)*

Pay special attention to the third-person singular and plural. In Spanish, two Spanish pronouns that express English "you"—**usted** and **ustedes**—are third-person pronouns rather than second-person pronouns. In Part Two, you will find detailed explanations about the different forms of Spanish pronouns for English "you."

The two-part overview of Spanish pronouns on the following two pages demonstrates classification by grammar person. The first chart explains singular pronouns, and the second chart explains plural pronouns.

Note that the third-person singular and plural is further divided into sections on persons and things.

Persons	Things

This is included to illustrate the contrast between the two groups. Specific examples will help you to better understand these concepts.

Note also that you will find no direct Spanish equivalent for the English pronoun *it*. All inanimate objects or things become either **él** (*he*) or **ella** (*she*).

The plural English pronoun *they* can be used for both persons and things, just like the two Spanish pronouns **ellos** and **ellas**.

Personal Pronouns

Grammar Person	Singular	
1 First-Person Pronoun	 Yo soy mexicana. *I am Mexican.*	A *first-person pronoun* is used in place of a speaker. **Yo** replaces **Maria**.
2 Second-Person Pronoun	 Tú eres mexicana. *You are Mexican.*	A *second-person pronoun* is used in place of a person spoken to. **Tú** replaces **Maria**.

	Person	Thing
	Used in place of a person or thing spoken about	
3 Third-Person Pronoun	**Él** replaces **Jake**, a male. Él nada. *He swims.* Anna talking about Jake	**Él** replaces **el colchón de aire**, a masculine inanimate object. Él es verde. *It is green.* Anna talking about the air mattress
	Ella replaces **Kelly**, a female. Ella es pequeña. *She is little.* Andy talking about Kelly	**Ella** replaces **la toalla**, a feminine inanimate object. Ella es pequeña. *It is little.* Andy talking about the towel
	Used in place of a person spoken to in a formal way	
	Usted replaces **Mr. Miller**, a person. Usted es amable. *You are kind.* Ben talking to one adult	**Usted** is never used to refer to things.

Personal Pronouns

Grammar Person	Plural

1 — First-Person Pronoun

Used in place of speakers

Nosotros somos americanos.

We are Americans.

Nosotros (masculine) replaces **Ben y Jake**; it includes the pronoun **yo** as the speaker.

Nosotras somos americanas.

We are Americans.

Nosotras (feminine) replaces **Anna y Susan**; it includes the pronoun **yo** as the speaker.

2 — Second-Person Pronoun

Note: **Vosotros/vosotras** is the informal form that expresses English "you" in the plural. These pronouns are used mainly in Spain and are not covered in this book.

3 — Third-Person Pronoun

Persons	Things

Used in place of persons or things spoken about

Ellos replaces **Ben y Jake**, two males.

Ellos nadan.

They swim.

Anna talking about Ben and Jake

Ellos replaces **los colchones de aire**, two masculine plural inanimate objects.

Ellos son verdes.

They are green.

Anna talking about the air mattresses

Ellas replaces **Anna y Susan**, two females.

Ellas nadan.

They swim.

Maria talking about Susan and Anna

Ellas replaces **las toallas**, two feminine plural inanimate objects.

Ellas son pequeñas.

They are little.

Andy talking about the towels

Persons: Ustedes

Used in place of persons spoken to in a formal way or as a group

Ustedes replaces **Mr. Miller y Mrs. Miller**, two people.

Ustedes son amables.

You are kind.

Ben talking to two adults

Ustedes replaces **Jake, Ben y Anna**, a group of friends.

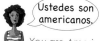

Ustedes son americanos.

You are Americans.

Maria talking to several friends

Think of a school with many floors. If floors were not labeled according to first, second, and third, etc., how would you know where to go? How could you find your way around? The same idea applies to grammar person. Organization is often the key to good learning. Grammar person will make frequent apperances in explanations and charts.

Next, we explain how the concepts of number and gender relate to pronouns.

3.5 Number of Spanish Personal Pronouns

The concept of number divides pronouns into groups of singular and plural pronouns. In the singular, the pronouns listed stand for one person or one thing only. In the plural, pronouns refer to more than one person or thing.

**The form of a personal pronoun
shows either singular or plural *number*.**

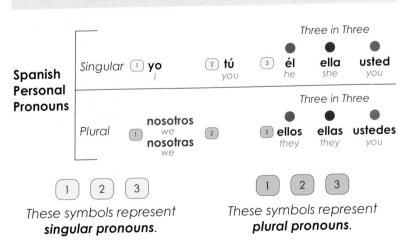

These symbols represent **singular pronouns**.

These symbols represent **plural pronouns**.

! *Hint: Be smart! Recognizing the number that a pronoun shows through its form is a great way to prepare for Chapter 4, Verbs.*

We now introduce a more detailed pronoun chart for your review.

Determining whether a pronoun is singular or plural is similar to determining whether a noun is singular or plural. Do you understand the difference between the pronoun standing for one person or thing and the pronoun standing for many? If so, you have a clear understanding of the number concept.

The yellow and orange symbols show six groups of personal pronouns.

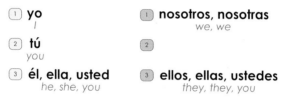

In this book, we do not cover the Spanish second-person plural pronouns as used in Spain. Therefore, they are not included in pronoun or verb charts.

Each of the following five symbols can be related to a different verb form. Would it make your job easier to know that each yellow symbol ① ② ③ takes a singular verb form and each orange symbol ① ③ connects to a plural verb form?

3.6 Gender of Spanish Personal Pronouns

The next chart is a general overview of singular and plural pronouns. Focus your attention on details about the gender of pronouns.

Learn to correctly identify masculine 🖈 and feminine 🖈 forms of pronouns for both singular and plural pronouns. It is essential information that determines the form of the verb as well as other parts of a sentence.

Singular Pronoun	Plural Pronoun	Explanations
① **yo** *I* yo	① **nosotros** *we* or **nosotras** *we*	*I* becomes *we* in the plural. **Nosotros** and **nosotras** both show gender.
② **tú** *you* tú		The pronoun **tú** is always written with an accent: **tú**. **Tú** shows no gender.
③ **él** *he* él	③ **ellos** *they* ellos	**Él** and **ella** in the singular and **ellos** and **ellas** in the plural show gender. *He* and *she* show gender in English, but the plural pronoun *they* does not.
ella *she* ella	**ellas** *they* ellas	
usted *you* (formal) usted	**ustedes** *you* (formal) ustedes	The formal forms of the Spanish pronoun for English "you," both singular (**usted**) and plural (**ustedes**), do not show gender.

Masculine forms of Spanish pronouns are *él, ellos,* and *nosotros.* Feminine forms of Spanish pronouns are *ella, ellas,* and *nosotras.*

Replacing Nouns with Third-Person Singular and Plural Pronouns

As the chart indicates, Spanish pronouns showing gender (in English, *he, she, we,* and *they*) can replace both singular and plural nouns.

Study the following overview of many nouns that third-person singular ③ and plural ③ pronouns can replace. Nouns are often used with other words in a phrase. We have highlighted the most important noun or nouns in each group of words. Focus your attention on the highlighted nouns.

People

Singular Masculine

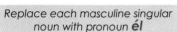

señor Miller
mi padre
su amigo Ben
el chico americano
el gerente de la piscina

*Replace each masculine singular noun with pronoun **él***

Singular Feminine

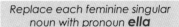

señora Miller
tu madre
esta chica
nuestra hija
la estudiante de intercambio

*Replace each feminine singular noun with pronoun **ella***

Plural Masculine

el señor Miller y el señor Smith
el señor Miller y Maria
Ben y Jake
los chicos mexicanos

*Replace each masculine plural noun, combination of masculine nouns, or combination of masculine and feminine nouns with pronoun **ellos***

Plural Feminine

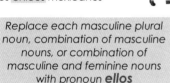

la señora Miller y Maria
mis amigas
Anna y Susan
las chicas inglesas

*Replace each feminine plural noun or combination of feminine nouns with pronoun **ellas***

Things

Singular Masculine

el sombrero
mi silbato
este perro caliente
su libro inglés

*Replace each masculine singular noun with pronoun **él***

Singular Feminine

la piscina
tu crema
mi hamburguesa
la fiesta americana

*Replace each feminine singular noun with pronoun **ella***

Plural Masculine

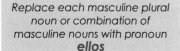

los zapatos
mis anteojos de sol
el sombrero y el silbato

*Replace each masculine plural noun or combination of masculine nouns with pronoun **ellos***

Plural Feminine

mi toalla y mi crema
las gafas de piscina
las fiestas americanas

*Replace each feminine plural noun or combination of feminine nouns with pronoun **ellas***

> **The English pronoun "it" has no Spanish equivalent.**
> **Use *él* or *ella*, depending on the gender**
> **of the singular noun it replaces.**
> **Replace a plural noun with either *ellos* or *ellas*.**

! *Hint: When replacing nouns with pronouns, remember how important gender is!*

Identifying the Gender of a Speaker

Other pronouns that indicate gender include **nosotros** and **nosotras**. These plural pronouns include the speaker. Remember: If you state *Mary and I,* you can replace the noun-pronoun combination with the single English pronoun *we.*

The pronoun *I* can refer to either a masculine or a feminine speaker. In Spanish, it is important to identify this speaker for the plural *we,* because you have a choice between **nosotros** (masculine) or **nosotras** (feminine). You must identify the gender of the speaker before you can select the correct form of the Spanish pronoun.

Here are two examples that show how the gender of the speaker determines the use of the Spanish pronoun for English "we."

Ben, a masculine noun, is replaced by the pronoun **yo**. When joining **Maria** and **yo**, the masculine form **nosotros** (*we*) applies.

Anna, a feminine noun, is replaced by the pronoun **yo**. When joining **Maria** and **yo**, the feminine form **nosotras** (*we*) applies.

This ends our section on personal pronouns based on form. Part Two will show how these pronouns become subjects in sentences.

3.7 Pronouns Pointing Out People or Things

A demonstrative pronoun points out people or things. Its distance from the speaker is expressed through different forms of the pronoun. Is the person or thing discussed near or far away? **Éste** or **ésta** is used for a person or thing close by, and **ése** or **ésa** for something farther away.

> A *demonstrative pronoun* is used to point out specific persons, places, or things.

Both demonstrative pronouns and demonstrative adjectives point out people or things. Demonstrative pronouns and adjectives have the same form except for the use of accents. When used as a pronoun, a demonstrative form must be marked with an accent and it stands alone.

The two examples that follow show the demonstrative pronouns used to represent things close by or farther away. The first example uses the feminine forms, because they replace **la hamburguesa**. **Ésta** and **ésa** are the feminine singular demonstrative pronouns. The second example uses the masculine forms, because they replace **el perro caliente**. **Éste** and **ése** are the masculine singular demonstrative pronouns.

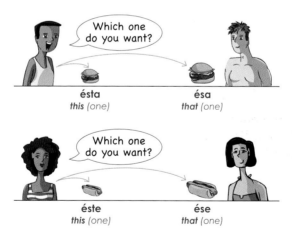

ésta	ésa
this (one)	*that (one)*

éste	ése
this (one)	*that (one)*

> **Spanish demonstrative pronouns show number and gender in their form.**

Look carefully at the following charts that show the demonstrative adjectives and their corresponding demonstrative pronouns.

Distance: Close to Speaker

Gender	Number	Demonstrative Adjective	Noun	Demonstrative Pronoun
Masculine	Singular	este chico		éste
	Plural	estos chicos		éstos
Feminine	Singular	esta chica		ésta
	Plural	estas chicas		éstas

Distance: Farther Away from the Speaker

Gender	Number	Demonstrative Adjective	Noun	Demonstrative Pronoun
Masculine	Singular	ese chico		ése
	Plural	esos chicos		ésos
Feminine	Singular	esa chica		ésa
	Plural	esas chicas		ésas

**Accent marks distinguish between demonstrative
pronouns and demonstrative adjectives.
Accents *must* be used on demonstrative pronouns.**

*! Hint: Replace a demonstrative adjective and its noun with the
demonstrative form alone, and then add the accent mark.
This will help you remember that pronouns stand alone.*

*Next we cover interrogative pronouns, which are commonly called
question words.*

3.8 Pronouns Forming Questions

Cómo (*how*), **cuál** (*which*), **cuánto** (*how much* or *how many*),
and **qué** (*what*) are common question words.

Question words are used to form questions. They can be used
to ask about people or things. In Spanish, they are called
las palabras interrogativas.

**An *interrogative pronoun*
is used to introduce a question.**

A question commonly asked by beginners is "What is this?" When asking this question in Spanish, a separate demonstrative pronoun is used: **esto**. It has no accent, and it does not indicate number or gender.

Qué is used to ask a question of a general nature. It relates to things only.

¿Qué es esto?
What is this?

You want to identify
an inanimate object.

esto
No accent / No number / No gender

The question word *qué* introduces a general question.

Qué is used to identify things; **quién** is used to identify people.

Here are two examples using the Spanish question word for English "who." Learn to distinguish between *who* and *what*.

¿Quién **nada**?
Who swims?

You want to identify
a person.

Quién (*who*) begins a question that asks for *one* person. The same question can take a plural form when it is used to identify several people.

¿Quiénes **nadan**?
Who swims?

You want to identify
more than one person.

English "who" does not distinguish between singular and plural. Spanish uses the singular **quién** and the plural **quiénes**.

The question word *quién* is singular in form.
***Quiénes* is plural in form.**
Both are used to identify persons only.

Quién can also be used in combination with other words. By adding the word **de** before **quién**, you are asking to identify *ownership*.

In the following example, the owner of the bathing suit is stated after the word **de**.

El traje de baño es de Ben.

The bathing suit belongs to Ben.

What if you want to find out whose bathing suit it is? *Whose*, the question word in English for ownership, is expressed in Spanish by using the combination **de quién**. In order to form a question that asks for ownership, you ask **¿De quién?** (*Of whom?* or *Whose?*).

Let's start with the following statement: **El traje de baño es de Ben.**

El traje de baño **es de** ___?___.
           | | |
     Possession *Verb* *Owner*

You want to identify ownership.

Now you want to form a question. Use **de** and the question word **quién** to identify ownership.

¿De quién es el traje de baño?

Whose bathing suit is it? is the most common English translation for this question. A literal translation of the question is *Of whom is the bathing suit?*

El traje de baño **es de** *Ben.*
           | | |
     Possession *Verb* *Owner*

You have identified the owner.

De quién **is used to identify ownership.**

We now move on to Part Two, the uses of pronouns.

PART TWO: USES OF SPANISH PRONOUNS
What Jobs Can Pronouns Do?

3.9 Introduction: "You" Alert

Languages may have the same origin, but evolve differently over time in different countries. The English spoken in England is not the same as the English spoken in the United States. The Spanish spoken in Spain is not the same as the Spanish spoken in Central and South America. One of the differences in the Spanish language concerns the form and use of pronouns. This chapter introduces pronouns as you will hear them spoken in countries close to North America.

How do you say "you" in Spanish? For the beginning language learner, the answer isn't as simple as it may seem. Spanish, like many other languages, has several different ways to address other people, all of which translate as the English word "you."

 In English, there is no formal "you." The same pronoun meaning "you" can be either formal or informal. It is therefore important that you learn to understand the distinction between formal and informal when using the different forms of the Spanish words for English "you."

The Spanish form used for English "you" depends on the person addressed and the circumstances.

It is important to learn the different Spanish words for English "you" and the proper uses of each. If you are not a native speaker, chances are no one will criticize you for using the wrong form, although you may be politely corrected.

Think of the contrast between these two situations: You would greet your teacher politely by asking "How are you today?" With your friends, a more relaxed exchange can take place: "What's up?"

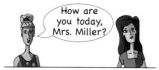

This difference between a formal and an informal exchange in conversation is reflected by the use of the Spanish pronouns **tú** and **usted**.

When you learn about the pronoun "you" in Spanish, the terms *formal* (or *polite*) and *informal* (or *familiar*) are used. These terms point out whether the Spanish forms for English "you" are being used in a formal or an informal way.

Let's start with details about the two singular Spanish pronouns that express English "you": **tú** *and* **usted**.

3.10 Singular Pronouns: *Tú* and *Usted*

Tú and **usted** are both singular pronouns that mean "you" in English.

The pronoun **tú** is used throughout Spain and Latin America for informal address. As the term *informal* indicates, this pronoun is used when addressing a close relative, a younger friend, or someone you know well. **Tú** is the equivalent of English "you" in the singular.

Here is an example of an English dialogue between two friends. You would use the pronoun **tú** where the English "you" appears.

Using the *tú* form

Ben: *Hey Jake! Are **you** going to Anna's party tonight?*
Jake: *Yes, are **you** going?*
Ben: *Yes, I am going with a friend.*
Jake: *Okay, see **you** tonight!*

Usted (abbreviated **Ud.**) is the formal, or polite, form for English "you." **Usted** is used when addressing one person politely or with formality, such as a teacher, the president, anyone with authority, all older persons, or any unknown person you meet.

In the following English dialogue, the response by the student is an example of the use of Spanish **usted**.

Using the *usted* form

Teacher: *Hello, I will be your teacher for today.*
Student: *Hi, it's nice to meet **you**.*
Teacher: *Please take your seat.*

The following examples illustrate two situations in which people might engage in conversation using the pronoun "you." The first example is an exchange between friends; they use the informal **tú**. The second example shows how the form **usted** is used to address an older adult or a person in authority.

Informal Friends and Family	Formal Adults or Persons in Authority

In the next two examples, the greeting "How are you?" shows how **tú** and **usted** are used to ask a question. In the first example, Maria asks Anna "How are you?" using the informal **tú** form. The second example shows Susan asking Mr. Smith "How are you?" using the formal pronoun **usted**.

Note that the two pronouns are used with different verb endings.

Informal "you"	Formal "you"

Tú and *usted* require different verb endings.

In this context, we refer to an important rule that will enhance your comprehension of the Spanish pronouns for English "you."

Singular: The "Three in Three" Rule Revisited

89

English and Spanish both have three pronouns in the third-person singular (see the section on grammar person). This basic concept is represented by ●●●. Since Spanish has no equivalent for *it,* you can think of the Spanish pronoun **usted** as the third pronoun in the Spanish third-person singular.

Singular Spanish Pronouns Expressing "You" Together with Verb Forms

② tú est**ás**	③ él est**á**	ella est**á**	usted est**á**
you are	*he is*	*she is*	*you are*

Tú and **usted** each has its own verb form.

> **"You are" = *tú estás***
> These pronoun and verb forms in both English and Spanish are in second-person singular. The English pronoun "you" is a direct correlation for the Spanish pronoun *tú.*
>
> **"You are" = *usted está***
> The Spanish pronoun *usted* is used with the third-person singular verb form, not the second-personal singular.

3.11 Plural Pronoun: *Ustedes*

In Latin America, **ustedes** (abbreviated **Uds.**) is used as the plural of both **tú** and **usted**. **Ustedes** is used for both formal and informal address when speaking to two or more people.

Here are examples that show two situations in which people might engage in conversation using the pronoun **ustedes**. The first example shows the use of **ustedes** (informal) between a son and his parents. The second example shows the use of **ustedes** (formal) when addressing adults or persons in authority.

Informal **Friends and Family**	**Formal** **Adults or Persons in Authority**

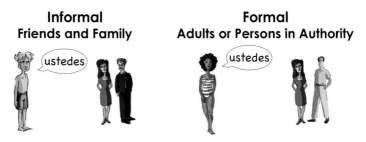

The Spanish pronoun *ustedes* serves a double function. It can be used in both formal and informal address.

We present the greetings again, this time in plural form. In the first example, Andy is asking "How are you?" using **ustedes** (informal) when talking to his friends. In the second example, Maria is asking the same question using **ustedes** (formal) when addressing older adults.

Informal Plural "you"

Formal Plural "you"

"You are" = *ustedes están*. **The Spanish pronoun *ustedes* is used with third-person plural verb forms.**

Plural Spanish Pronouns Expressing "You" with Verb Forms

Ellos, **ellas**, and **ustedes** share the same verb form.

In summary, we illustrate the three different forms of English "you"—**tú**, **usted**, and **ustedes**—one more time. Note that each pronoun uses a different verb form.

Tú, **usted**, *and* **ustedes** *are all subject pronouns. We continue with other subject pronouns needed to build sentences.*

3.12 A Great Start: Using Subject Pronouns

When a personal pronoun is connected to a verb, it becomes a *subject pronoun*. A subject pronoun connected to a verb forms a *unit*. This unit is the most basic sentence you can build.

> **Pronouns are either singular or plural.**
> **Verb forms are either singular or plural.**

Here is an English example that shows a unit with a subject and a verb.

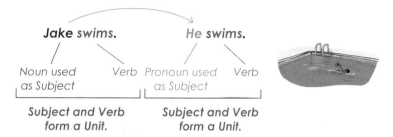

Jake *swims.*   *He swims.*

Noun used   Verb   Pronoun used   Verb
as Subject   as Subject

Subject and Verb   **Subject and Verb**
form a Unit.   **form a Unit.**

Jake, the subject, is a *building block.* When replacing the name *Jake* with the pronoun *he,* the pronoun is also a building block. In order to label *Jake* or *he* as the subject, the noun or pronoun needs to perform the action of a verb, in this case, *swims.* When the two elements—the subject and the verb—are connected, you will have formed a complete unit, or sentence.

The subject in a unit can be either singular or plural.

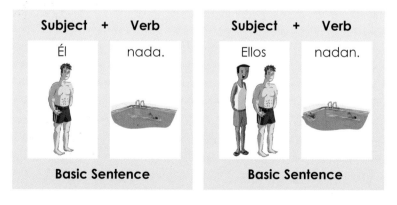

Subject	+	Verb		Subject	+	Verb
Él		nada.		Ellos		nadan.
Basic Sentence				**Basic Sentence**		

> **A singular pronoun used as a subject requires**
> **a verb in singular form. A plural pronoun**
> **must be connected to a verb in plural form.**

92

Pronouns have many jobs to do. You already know that subject pronouns *perform* the action of the verb. We will now introduce pronouns that *receive* the action of the verb.

3.13 Overview of Subject and Direct Object Pronouns

Consider the following overview. It lists both subject and direct object pronouns so that you can see the difference.

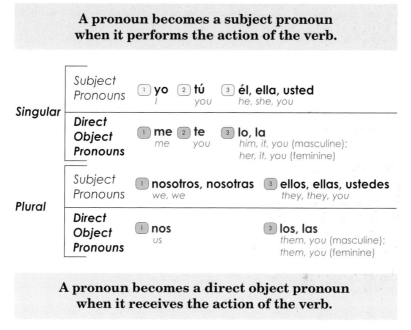

**A pronoun becomes a subject pronoun
when it performs the action of the verb.**

	Subject Pronouns	① **yo** *I*	② **tú** *you*	③ **él, ella, usted** *he, she, you*
Singular	Direct Object Pronouns	① **me** *me*	② **te** *you*	③ **lo, la** *him, it, you (masculine); her, it, you (feminine)*
	Subject Pronouns	① **nosotros, nosotras** *we, we*		③ **ellos, ellas, ustedes** *they, they, you*
Plural	Direct Object Pronouns	① **nos** *us*		③ **los, las** *them, you (masculine); them, you (feminine)*

**A pronoun becomes a direct object pronoun
when it receives the action of the verb.**

Find out how direct object pronouns are used in context.

3.14 Direct Object Pronouns

You have seen how the verbs **comer** 🍔 and **amar** ♥ expand to include nouns as direct objects. Some of these examples are repeated in this chapter. They show how nouns form the basis for pronoun replacements.

The last two examples in this section introduce the verb **llamar** (*to call (someone by phone)*). ☎

Direct Object Pronouns

Singular Pronouns   **Plural Pronouns**

Symbols Indicate *Gender* of Pronouns

me	te	lo	la	nos	los	las
me	*you*	*him, it, you* (masculine)	*her, it, you* (feminine)	*us*	*them, you* (masculine)	*them, you* (feminine)

One in Number   *More Than One in Number*

The Division Indicates *Number* of Pronouns

As the chart above shows, the classification of number and gender that was introduced with subject pronouns in the previous section also applies to direct object pronouns. **Lo** (*him*), **la** (*her*), **los** (*them*), and **las** (*them*) show gender.

> **Nouns used as direct objects can be replaced by direct object pronouns *lo* or *la* (singular), *los* or *las* (plural).**

Consider this English sentence: *The boy eats. The boy eats* represents a unit. It can stand alone. The subject is the noun *boy*. *The boy* performs the action of the verb *eats*. By adding *a hot dog* (a noun with an article) after the verb, you extend the unit to include a direct object. *A hot dog* is now your direct object. *A hot dog* receives the action of the verb. As a building block, it is not able to stand alone. By connecting subject, verb, and direct object, you form an extended unit. Your sentence now has a subject, a verb, and a direct object: *The boy eats a hot dog.*

When *Lo* Expresses the English Pronoun "It"

Here is the English example above illustrated in Spanish.

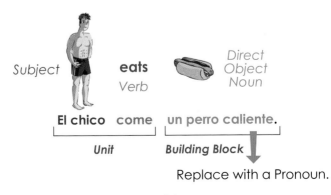

94

In this example, there are two different nouns. The noun **chico** is the subject and the noun **perro caliente** is the direct object.

> **Identify the number and gender of each Spanish noun used as a direct object. Object pronouns match the number and gender of the nouns they replace.**

The following description will explain the steps you must take when replacing the direct object, **un perro caliente**, with a pronoun.

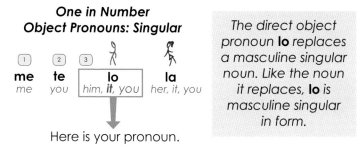

One in Number
Object Pronouns: Singular

me	te	lo	la
me	you	him, **it**, you	her, it, you

Here is your pronoun.

*The direct object pronoun **lo** replaces a masculine singular noun. Like the noun it replaces, **lo** is masculine singular in form.*

Number: **Perro caliente** is a noun in singular form.
Gender: **Perro caliente** is a noun in masculine form.
Grammar Person: Noun replacement is found in third-person singular.

> **Direct objects, either as nouns or pronouns, receive the action of the verb.**

The direct object pronoun **lo** can be used to replace the noun **un perro caliente**.

El chico lo come.

Subject   Direct   Verb
           Object
           Pronoun
The boy eats it.

Note the placement of the pronoun. In Spanish, direct object pronouns are placed *before* the verb. **Lo** is placed *before* the verb **come**.

The next example shows how to replace a masculine singular noun that names a person. Learn to recognize the shift in meaning from *it* to *him*.

When *Lo* Expresses the English Pronoun "Him"

My sister loves **her dad**.

My sister loves **him**.

Mi hermana ama su padre.

Subject — Verb — Personal **a** — *Direct Object*

Mi hermana lo ama.

Subject — *Direct Object* — Verb

Learn to identify the **Subject**. Who is performing the action?

Learn to identify the **Direct Object**. Who is receiving the action? If a person receives the action, remember to use the **personal a**.

One in Number
Object Pronouns: Singular

①	②	③		
me	**te**		**lo**	**la**
me	*you*		***him***, *it, you*	*her, it, you*

Learn to identify **Number**. Is it a singular or a plural noun? Learn to identify **Gender**. Is it a masculine or a feminine noun?

If you identified **su padre** as a masculine singular noun, you are well prepared to find the matching pronoun. The personal **a** together with the noun **su padre** are replaced by the direct object pronoun **lo**, a *third-person masculine* (gender) *singular* (number) pronoun. **Lo** is placed *before* the verb.

> **Spanish direct object pronouns are placed *before* the verb.**

The same concepts used with singular pronouns apply to this plural example.

Los chicos comen las hamburguesas.

Subject — Verb — *Direct Object*

Los chicos las comen.

Subject — *Direct Object* — Verb

More Than One in Number
Object Pronouns: Plural

① **nos**	③ **los**	**las**
us	***them**, you*	***them**, you*

Las is the direct object pronoun that is feminine and plural in form. It is a third-person plural pronoun.

Both sentences are illustrated below. The sentence on the left includes the plural noun **las hamburguesas** as a direct object. The sentence on the right shows replacement of the noun with the pronoun **las** as the direct object pronoun in plural form. Note its placement before the verb **comen**.

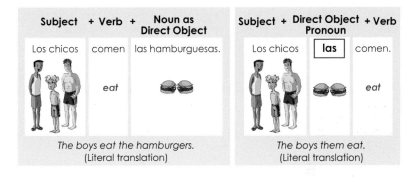

Subject	+ Verb +	Noun as Direct Object
Los chicos	comen	las hamburguesas.
	eat	

The boys eat the hamburgers.
(Literal translation)

Subject +	Direct Object Pronoun	+ Verb
Los chicos	**las**	comen.
		eat

The boys them eat.
(Literal translation)

Let's introduce another verb commonly used with direct object pronouns: **llamar**. **Llamar** means *to call*.

Mi madre **me** llama.

My mother calls me.

Mi madre **nos** llama.

My mother calls us.

! *Hint: Memorize the forms of pronouns just like you memorize vocabulary words.*

Let's move on to pronouns that follow a preposition.

3.15 A Different Job: Object Pronouns with Prepositions

Just as in English, prepositions in Spanish are followed by an object, either in the form of a noun or a pronoun.

Pronouns used as objects of a preposition are called *prepositional pronouns*.

Most of the Spanish pronouns used with prepositions are the same as the subject pronouns. They show a different form only in first- and second-person singular. Otherwise, their use is fairly straightforward.

The following chart uses the preposition **para** (*for*) with all prepositional pronouns.

	Singular		Plural	
	Preposition	Prepositional Pronoun	Preposition	Prepositional Pronoun
	para for	**mí** me	para for	nosotros nosotras us/ourselves
Informal	para for	**ti** you		
Formal Form	para for	usted you	para for	ustedes you
	para for	él him	para for	ellos them
	para for	ella her	para for	ellas them

**The two special forms of prepositional pronouns
are *mí* and *ti*. Subject pronouns serve
as all other prepositional pronouns.**

3.16 Details About Chapter Sequence

Congratulations! You've completed the chapter on pronouns.
We hope that you used this chapter as an opportunity to review
what you already knew about nouns and pronouns, as well as
to build on your knowledge of the Spanish language.

Together, the first three chapters—on nouns, adjectives, and
pronouns—give you a strong foundation upon which to add
verbs. Now that you know the two types of words (nouns and
pronouns) that you can use as subjects, you are ready to make
those subjects come to life in complete sentences.

The next chapter will teach you the skills you need to form
a grammatically correct unit, or sentence. By stressing the
difference between singular and plural subjects in the pronoun
chapter, the groundwork is laid for an easy transition to verbs.
With your thorough knowledge of subjects, matching a subject
to the correct verb will be easy!

You are now ready to begin Chapter 4, Verbs.

3.17 Spanish Pronoun Practice

These short, conversational exchanges stress the use of the Spanish pronouns **tú**, **usted**, and **ustedes**. Use the names of persons to help you analyze the form of address used, either informal or formal.

For each dialogue, write the Spanish pronoun(s) expressing "you" on the first line; write *informal* or *formal* on the second line, depending on your analysis of the form of address used.

Dialogue 1:

Ben: Hola. *Hi.*
Susan, Maria y Anna: Hola.
Ben: ¿Cómo están ustedes?
Susan: Muy bien, gracias. *Very well, thanks.*
Maria: Estoy bien, gracias. *I am doing well, thanks.*
Anna: Bien, gracias. ¿Y tú? *Well, thanks. And you?*
Ben: Muy bien. *Very well.*

Dialogue 2:

Jake: Buenas tardes. *Good afternoon.*
Andy: Hola. *Hi.*
Jake: ¿Cómo estás tú?
Andy: Bien, gracias. ¿Y tú? *Well, thanks. And you?*
Jake: Muy bien. *Very well.*

Dialogue 3:

Señor Miller: Buenos días. *Good day.*
Maria: ¿Cómo está usted?
Señor Miller: Muy bien, gracias. *Very well, thanks.*

CHAPTER 4

VERBS

4.1 Part One and Part Two Overview   102

PART ONE: VERB BASICS
4.2 Verb Families, Regular Verbs, and Verb Stems   102
4.3 English and Spanish Subject-Verb Connection   107
4.4 Stem-Changing Verbs   118
4.5 Irregular Verbs   118
4.6 Spanish Helping Verb **Estar**   121
4.7 Reflexive Verbs: Stating Names   122

PART TWO: VERBS IN USE
4.8 Verb Tenses: Verbs Express Time   123
4.9 Using **Gustar**   136
4.10 Using **Hay**   137
4.11 Details About Chapter Sequence   138
4.12 Verb Grids for Conjugation Practice   140
4.13 Spanish Subject-Verb Connection Practice   147

4.1 Part One and Part Two Overview

> **The *verb* is the most fundamental part of speech.**
> **Only verbs can make a statement about the subject.**

Verbs play the central part in a sentence. Without a verb, nothing would happen!

Understanding the process of connecting a subject to a verb is the focus in Part One. We call this the *subject-verb connection*.

In Part Two, the subject-verb connection will be further developed in the presentations of verb conjugations and verb tenses. Because this book is concerned with just the basics of Spanish grammar, only a few verb tenses are included.

A solid understanding of verb tenses requires examples in context. The example that follows introduces three situations involving the exchange student Maria. Several examples in Part Two draw upon these situations to illustrate the basic verb tenses, questions and answers, and verbs used in commands.

Now	Tomorrow	Yesterday
Planning a Trip	Upcoming Events	Past Events

=== Mexico! ===

I am planning a trip to Miami.

I will be here.

I had a great trip.

PART ONE: VERB BASICS

4.2 Verb Families, Regular Verbs, and Verb Stems

Verb Families

We begin the chapter with a list of verbs that appear throughout the chapter. Visual representations of verbs through graphic images will help you associate specific Spanish verbs with their meaning. Use this list to make the connection between the image and the verb it represents.

nadar *to swim*	**celebrar** *to celebrate*	**leer** *to read*	**amar** *to love*	**comer** *to eat*	**vivir** *to live*
visitar *to visit*	**escribir** *to write*	**entrar** *to enter*	**hablar** *to speak*	**ir** *to go*	**llamar** *to call*

Verb basics start with verb families.

A family's name is important to any family. It includes all the members of that family. Verbs also have families. Each verb family has many different parts that belong within the family. In grammar, we call the family name of a verb its *infinitive form.*

The Miller Family

In English, an infinitive is identified by the word "to" in front of the verb. Examples include *to eat, to swim, to write,* and *to love.*

to eat	to swim	to write	to love
com**er**	nad**ar**	escrib**ir**	am**ar**

> **All Spanish verb families belong to one of three groups, depending on the verb ending. In Spanish, an infinitive is identified by its ending: *-ar, -er,* or *-ir.***

In Spanish, the infinitive form of a verb is identified by its ending. There are three groups of verbs. Within these three verb groups, verbs that follow a predictable pattern are called *regular verbs.* This introduction continues with a detailed explanation of these predictable patterns.

Regular Verbs

-ar Verbs

The first group is composed of verbs ending in **-ar**.

nad**ar** *to swim*	celebr**ar** *to celebrate*	estudi**ar** *to study*	am**ar** *to love*
entr**ar** *to enter*	habl**ar** *to speak*	visit**ar** *to visit*	llam**ar** *to call*

Verbs in this group show a common pattern: The forms they take apply to all regular verbs that end in **-ar**. This group of verbs is the largest, so they are used extensively in this chapter.

-er Verbs

The second group of verbs is composed of verbs ending in **-er**.

com**er**
to eat

le**er**
to read

We will use only two examples of this verb family in the chapter: **comer** (*to eat*) and **leer** (*to read*). Verbs in this group show a common pattern: The forms they take apply to all regular verbs that end in **-er**.

This second group is not as large as the group of verbs ending in **-ar**. The verb **comer** (*to eat*) is frequently used throughout this chapter.

-ir Verbs

The third verb group is composed of verbs ending in **-ir**.

escribir
to write

vivir
to live

We will use only two examples from this verb group in the chapter: **escribir** (*to write*) and **vivir** (*to live*). Verbs in this group show a common pattern: The forms that they take apply to all regular verbs that end in **-ir**.

! Hint: Develop good habits! Knowing the three verb groups is important. Memorize each verb in its infinitive form.

Now we will summarize the three groups of Spanish verbs. The infinitive form of verbs in the first group ends in **-ar**, the infinitive of the second group in **-er**, and the infinitive of the third group in **-ir**.

-*ar* Verbs   -*er* Verbs   -*ir* Verbs

habl<u>ar</u>   com<u>er</u>   escrib<u>ir</u>

Note the underlined part of the three infinitives above: This is the *verb stem*. In illustrations and verb charts throughout the chapter, each verb stem will be underlined. In contrast, a verb form that is built on the infinitive will appear with a gray box.

Verb Stems

Recognizing the three different verb groups is the first important step toward understanding the basics of Spanish verbs. Verb groups in Spanish are identified by the verb endings **-ar**, **-er**, **-ir**. When the verb endings are removed, you are left with what is called the verb stem. Compare the stem to a skeleton to which you add all the parts necessary to form a complete body. Each skeleton is unique. When physical features are added to it, each body will be different. The same concept applies to verb stems. The stem can show variations. It can also be expanded in various ways, such as for *I study*:

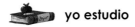 **yo estudio**

We focus on the stems of regular verbs for each of the three verb groups. Details on variations of the stem itself follow later in the chapter.

Six of the most common **-ar** verbs are illustrated next. Each verb is listed with its infinitive form and its stem.

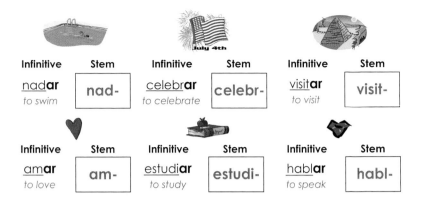

Note: For certain verbs like **estudiar**, the stem ends in a vowel. You must pay attention to vowels when studying Spanish verbs.

> **For all three verb groups, the verb stem is what remains when you remove the ending *-ar, -er,* or *-ir* from the infinitive form of the verb.**

Examples of verb infinitives and their verb stems are shown below for each of the three groups.

The stem of a regular verb is the base to which you add endings. Let's continue with a detailed description of this process.

> **A *verb* is a word that describes what the subject of a sentence does.**

Verbs need subjects to perform their actions. Therefore, verbs and subjects are closely connected. This process of joining subjects to matching verb forms is the most important part of this chapter. We call this the *subject-verb connection.* This process is also called *conjugation.* That term will be used in Part Two with the introduction of tenses. For now, we prefer the term subject-verb connection.

We will now focus on a detailed description of the subject-verb connection. Once you understand this process, we will add the concept of time expressed by a verb.

4.3 English and Spanish Subject-Verb Connection

Let's start with a short review of the subject-verb connection for an English verb. A firm English foundation provides a better understanding of the concept of subject-verb connection in Spanish.

English Subject-Verb Connection

In English, the *base form* of a verb is similar to the stem of a Spanish verb. The base form of an English verb is what you start with when connecting a verb to a subject; it has no endings added to it.

Verb Infinitive: *to swim*
Base form of Verb: *swim*

You are already familiar with grammar person. Review the modified statement below from Chapter 3, Pronouns.

The Importance of Grammar Person

The relationship between pronouns and verbs is important when building sentences. Before using verbs correctly, you must be able to understand the categories of pronouns based on grammar person. In Chapter 4, Verbs, we explain how the pattern of grammar person extends to the use of the different verb forms.

Continue with the next step: Add the correct verb form to each subject pronoun.

The following chart is divided into three columns. The left column gives the subject in the form of a pronoun. The middle column shows the form of the verb *to swim* after it connects to the subject. The third column provides the explanation necessary to understand the resulting changes.

Subject as Pronoun	Connecting Verb	Explanation
① I **I** *Person speaking*	swim	There are no verb changes in the first-person singular.
② You **you** *Person spoken to*	swim	There are no verb changes in the second-person singular.
③ **he** **she** **it** *Person or thing spoken about*	**swims**	There are verb changes in the third-person singular only. In English, add **-s** to the verb's base form.
① We **we** *People speaking*	swim	There are no verb changes in the first-person plural.
② You **you** *People spoken to*	swim	There are no verb changes in the second-person plural.
③ **they** *People or things spoken about*	swim	There are no verb changes in the third-person plural.

! *Hint: You may have noticed that there are only two English verb forms in the chart above:* **swim** *and* **swims**. *Spanish verb forms are more extensive. Be prepared!*

Most English verbs follow a similar pattern, though there may be minor spelling changes. In English, many different pronouns can connect to the same verb form. Subject pronouns must be stated, because otherwise we do not know who or what the subject is. In contrast, Spanish subject pronouns can often be omitted.

Become familiar with verb charts. They give you important details about the subject-verb connection. Refer to the subject-verb connection chart for the verb *to walk* on the next page.

English Verb *to walk*

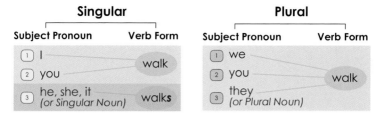

Singular		Plural	
Subject Pronoun	Verb Form	Subject Pronoun	Verb Form
① I	walk	① we	walk
② you		② you	
③ he, she, it (or Singular Noun)	walks	③ they (or Plural Noun)	

In English, as in Spanish, the subject and verb must match.

Spanish Subject-Verb Connection

After this brief overview of English subject-verb connection, you are now ready to learn about Spanish subject-verb connection.

Let's begin with three Spanish sentences. Focus your attention on the different verb endings.

Subject	Verb Stem	Verb Ending	
Ben y Jake *Ben and Jake*	nad	**an**. *swim.*	
Ben *Ben*	com	**e** *eats*	una hamburguesa. *a hamburger.*
Anna *Anna*	am	**a** *loves*	a su mamá. *her mother.*

Next we will explain the use of different Spanish verb endings.

Subject-Verb Connection: -*ar* Verbs

The process of combining a subject with a matching verb form will be explained in three steps. The first and second steps illustrate the subject-verb connection in a general way. Step three concludes with a general overview.

The verb **nadar** (*to swim*) takes center stage, with the stem **nad-** as your base. This is the middle section of the illustration and is your starting point. A section added to each side explains the parts that need to be connected. The subject section on the left side represents the *doer* of the action. The right section shows the verb form that matches your chosen subject.

First Step: Setting the Stage for the Verb *nadar*

Start Here

| Who is the *doer* of the action? | Verb Stem **nad-** | Which verb form matches the *doer*? |

add · choose one · add · choose one

Make a Match

Your task is learning how to make this match! Your choices for the *doer* (left side) are pronouns or nouns used as subjects. The pronoun chapter has prepared you well for this transition to verbs.

Review the charts showing pronouns based on grammar person. You will now learn how each pronoun extends to include a corresponding verb form based on grammar person.

Second Step: Specific Examples

After selecting the subject, add a personal ending to the stem of the verb.
This personal ending is based on the subject.

Next, the center-stage verb stem **nad-** is combined with (1) a specific subject and (2) a specific verb ending that corresponds to the subject. The pronoun **yo** (*I*) is placed in the box on the left. The box on the right shows the matching verb form **nado**.

Subject-Verb Connection

Subject Pronoun	Verb Stem	Verb Form
① yo	**nad-**	① nad**o**
②		②
③		③

yo nado
I swim

Verb endings tell who is doing the action. They change according to the *subject,* or *doer,* of the action.

Yo, the first-person singular pronoun, is the subject pronoun that combines with the verb form **nado**. The verb ending **-o** matches the subject **yo**.

The next two examples use two different subjects: a third-person singular subject and a third-person plural subject. This time there are two sentences at the end of each example. The first sentence uses a pronoun as the subject. The sentence is then repeated with a noun in place of the pronoun.

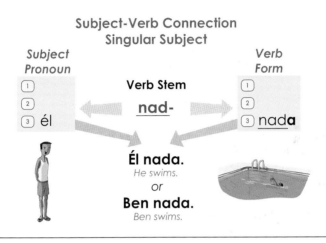

Subject-Verb Connection
Singular Subject

Él nada.
He swims.
or
Ben nada.
Ben swims.

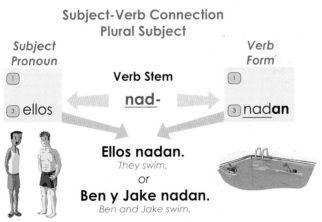

Subject-Verb Connection
Plural Subject

Ellos nadan.
They swim.
or
Ben y Jake nadan.
Ben and Jake swim.

Ben and **él** are both singular subjects. Either the name **Ben** or the pronoun **él** can be matched with the singular verb ending **-a**. **Ben y Jake** is a plural subject, and **ellos** is the plural pronoun that replaces the two names. Whether the plural subject is **Ben y Jake** or **ellos**, the verb ending is **-an**.

You have a choice when selecting your subject: It can be a noun or a pronoun. As the examples have shown, the verb ending is the same whether you choose the noun or the pronoun that replaces it. Refer to Chapter 3, Pronouns, to review full details on how pronouns take the place of nouns.

The verb charts in this chapter are based on pronouns.

Third Step: A Match for All Subject Pronouns

**A subject and its matching verb form
agree in person and number.**

The verb chart on the following page illustrates the subject-verb connection. It includes all subject pronouns and their matching verb forms with personal verb endings. This chart shows the subject-verb connection for the verb **nadar**. It shows the present tense. You will learn more about tenses in Part Two.

Verb charts in this book are based on the Spanish spoken in Latin America. The second-person plural forms (used only in Spain) are therefore omitted from the charts.

The overview of **nadar** includes three English meanings for each Spanish verb form. Note that we present the two singular "you" forms (**tú** and **usted**) together.

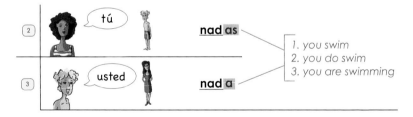

Tú and **usted** both mean "you" and share the same English translation. A closer look at the two Spanish verb forms, however, shows that the Spanish verb forms are different.

Comprehension of this fundamental Spanish grammar concept is the focus of several sections in this chapter. You will have numerous opportunities to reinforce your understanding of the difference between the various ways to express English "you" in Spanish.

Overview: Matching Subject Pronouns with Verb Forms

Verb: *nadar*

Subject Pronoun +	Verb Stem/Verb Endings	English Meaning

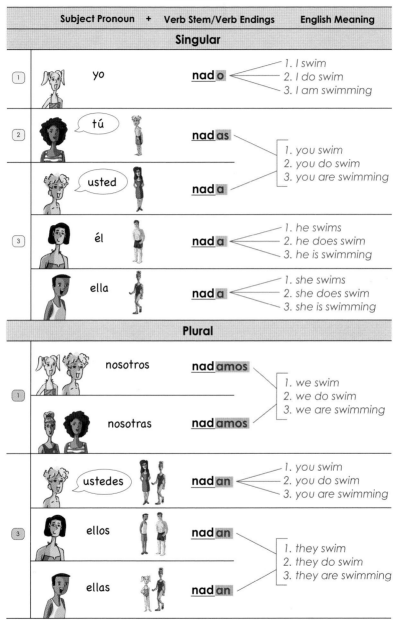

Singular

1. yo — nad**o**
  1. I swim
  2. I do swim
  3. I am swimming

2. tú — nad**as**
  usted — nad**a**
  1. you swim
  2. you do swim
  3. you are swimming

3. él — nad**a**
  1. he swims
  2. he does swim
  3. he is swimming

  ella — nad**a**
  1. she swims
  2. she does swim
  3. she is swimming

Plural

1. nosotros — nad**amos**
  nosotras — nad**amos**
  1. we swim
  2. we do swim
  3. we are swimming

  ustedes — nad**an**
  1. you swim
  2. you do swim
  3. you are swimming

3. ellos — nad**an**
  ellas — nad**an**
  1. they swim
  2. they do swim
  3. they are swimming

Each Spanish verb form matches subject pronouns in both singular forms ① ② ③ and plural forms ① ③. There are five different sets of pronouns, so there are five different personal verb endings to learn for each regular **-ar** verb.

*Hint: Learning Spanish personal verb endings is a **must**!*

How Subject Pronouns Relate to Verb Forms

What Person Means

Person indicates pronouns relating to people: **yo, tú, él, ella, usted, nosotros, nosotras, ellos, ellas**, and **ustedes**. They are called *personal pronouns*. When connected to Spanish verbs, each personal pronoun must match the verb form's personal verb ending.

What Number of Pronoun Means

The term *number* indicates the division of pronouns into singular and plural pronouns. The same concept applies to verbs: Number divides verbs into singular and plural verb forms.

What Choices for Pronouns Mean

Yo and **tú** each stands alone as the only pronoun that can be used with its specific verb form. In the third-person singular and plural, however, you have a choice of three pronouns for each verb form.

Three Forms of Singular Pronouns	Three Forms of Plural Pronouns
Subject (Singular) *Verb Form* (Singular)	*Subject* (Plural) *Verb Form* (Plural)
③ **usted** (*you*)	③ **ustedes** (*you*)
él (*he*) ⟶ one verb form	**ellos** (*they*) ⟶ one verb form
ella (*she*)	**ellas** (*they*)

Remember the "Three in Three" rule for Spanish third-person singular pronouns. There is only one verb form, but it can be combined with any of three pronouns: **usted**, **él**, or **ella**.	Remember the "Three in Three" rule for Spanish third-person plural pronouns. There is only one verb form, but it can be combined with any of three pronouns: **ustedes**, **ellos**, or **ellas**.

The singular pronouns **usted**, **él**, and **ella** can all be connected to the same Spanish verb form. It does not work the same way in English. In English, *he* and *she* connect to the same English verb form, but the pronoun *you* must be matched with a different verb form.

Three Spanish Pronouns	One Spanish Verb Form	Two English Translations
③ usted		you swim
él	nada	
ella		he/she swims

English translations in verb charts like the one above combine *he* and *she,* since they share the same verb form. The English translation for **usted** is listed separately. In the third-person plural, pronouns for both Spanish and English share the same verb form.

The following chart illustrates the subject-verb connection for the verb **nadar** with all subject pronouns and matching verb endings. It is the conjugation of the verb **nadar** in the present tense. More details about tenses follow in Part Two.

Verb: *nadar* (to swim)

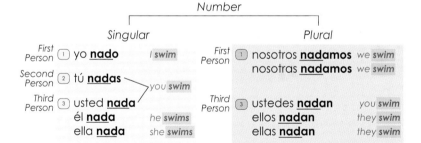

Number

Singular			Plural		
First Person ①	yo **nado**	I swim	First Person ①	nosotros **nadamos**	we swim
				nosotras **nadamos**	we swim
Second Person ②	tú **nadas**	you swim			
Third Person ③	usted **nada**		Third Person ③	ustedes **nadan**	you swim
	él **nada**	he swims		ellos **nadan**	they swim
	ella **nada**	she swims		ellas **nadan**	they swim
Personal Verb Endings	-o, -as, -a		Personal Verb Endings	-amos, -an	

It is important to understand first, second, and third person in both singular and plural. If asked "What is the verb form for the second-person singular of the verb **nadar**?" you would answer "**tú nadas.**"

Here is a rule that summarizes the subject-verb connection with **-ar** verbs.

> **To connect a subject pronoun to a regular -*ar* verb, drop the -*ar* ending and replace it with the personal verb ending that matches the subject.**

Check your progress. Does this statement make sense now?

Your task is to correctly connect a subject and a verb. It is an enormous task for beginners, but it is an important one to master.

! *Hint: You are a beginner. Learn to be patient! Verbs are a part of speech that requires a lot of memorization!*

Be proud to have learned that all regular verbs with **-ar** endings follow the same pattern.

Subject-Verb Connection: -*er* Verbs

You have been introduced to the verb endings of regular **-ar** verbs. The way you use **-ar** verbs in the subject-verb connection also applies to regular **-er** and **-ir** verbs. You simply use a new set of personal endings for each new group.

The five different verb forms of **comer** (*to eat*) are illustrated with the image of a hot dog. Note the personal verb endings for each verb in the bun of the hot dog.

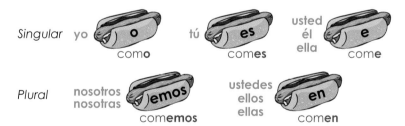

Singular yo **o**	tú **es**	usted él **e** ella
	com**o**	com**es**	com**e**
Plural nosotros nosotras **emos**	ustedes ellos **en** ellas	
	com**emos**	com**en**	

Subject-Verb Connection: -*ir* Verbs

Following are the five different verb forms of **escribir** (*to write*). Note the personal verb endings for each verb in the pencil.

A chart summarizing personal verb endings with all three groups of personal verb endings appears below.

Each group of regular verbs has its own set of personal verb endings.

Personal Verb Endings of All Three Groups

Subject Pronouns	*nadar* -ar	*comer* -er	*escribir* -ir
Singular			
① **yo** *I*	nad**o** swim	com**o** eat	escrib**o** write
② **tú** *you*	nad**as** swim	com**es** eat	escrib**es** write
③ **usted, él, ella** *you* *he, she*	nad**a** swim swims	com**e** eat eats	escrib**e** write writes
Plural			
① **nosotros, nosotras** *we, we*	nad**amos** swim	com**emos** eat	escrib**imos** write
③ **ustedes, ellos, ellas** *you, they, they*	nad**an** swim	com**en** eat	escrib**en** write

To connect a subject pronoun to a regular verb, drop the *-ar*, *-er*, or *-ir* ending and replace it with the personal verb ending that matches the subject.

Learn the personal verb endings for **-ar**, **-er**, and **-ir** verbs.

Hint: Connecting a subject to a verb is like multiplying two numbers together: Once you know how to do multiplication, you can multiply any numbers using the same concept.

4.4 Stem-Changing Verbs

Certain verbs within each group of regular verbs show specific patterns of changes. It is important to understand where these changes occur. The personal verb endings that you have learned for regular verbs still apply. However, they are now added to verb stems that show different forms.

Here we contrast the stem of the regular verb **hablar** (*to speak*) with the stems of the stem-changing verbs **pensar** (*to think*) and **dormir** (*to sleep*).

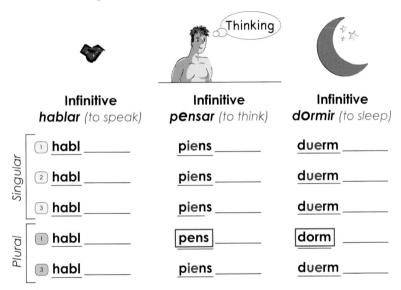

	Infinitive *hablar* (to speak)	Infinitive *pensar* (to think)	Infinitive *dormir* (to sleep)
Singular	① habl _____	piens _____	duerm _____
	② habl _____	piens _____	duerm _____
	③ habl _____	piens _____	duerm _____
Plural	① habl _____	pens _____	dorm _____
	③ habl _____	piens _____	duerm _____

Add the personal verb endings to the stem shown for each verb. The changes only occur in the stem itself. Do you notice that the vowel of the infinitive is kept in the first-person plural? All other verb forms change the vowel.

Hint: Be mindful of vowels—they play a central part with Spanish verbs.

In spite of the changes in the stem, these verbs add regular personal verb endings. The next verbs we will study are different.

4.5 Irregular Verbs

Let's briefly compare an irregular English verb to a regular English verb.

Regular Verb: A Pattern to Follow
Verb: to walk

Subject Pronoun	Regular Form
(1) I	
	walk
(2) you	
(3) he, she, it (or Singular Noun)	walks
(1) we	
(2) you	walk
(3) they (or Plural Noun)	

Irregular Verb: No Pattern to Follow
Verb: to be

Subject Pronoun	Irregular Form
(1) I	am
(2) you	are
(3) he, she, it (or Singular Noun)	is
(1) we	
(2) you	are
(3) they (or Plural Noun)	

The verb *to walk* is a regular verb. There are only two verb forms: *walk* and *walks*. The verb *to be* is an *irregular verb*. Its verb forms follow an unpredictable pattern. The verb forms *am, are,* and *is* are all part of the same verb.

> **Irregular verbs show different forms that require memorization.**

There is no easy pattern to learn for irregular verbs. If English is your mother tongue, you learned the various forms of the irregular verbs in English over many years of speaking the language.

Two of the most important verbs in Spanish are both irregular; they are introduced next.

Irregular Verbs *Estar* and *Ser*

Spanish has two different verbs, **estar** and **ser**, that correspond to the English verb *to be*. You will learn the differences in usage between **estar** and **ser** in Part Two. For now, focus on the forms of these and other irregular verbs.

The Spanish verb **estar** *(to be)* looks like a regular verb in the **-ar** group. However, **estar** is an irregular verb. Unlike regular verbs, the verb **estar** does not follow a predictable pattern.

The following verb charts list the verb forms for **estar** and **ser**.

estar: to be

Singular		Plural	
① yo **estoy**	I am	① nosotros/nosotras **estamos**	we are
② tú **estás**	you are		
③ usted **está**		③ ustedes **están**	you are
③ él/ella **está**	he/she is	③ ellos/ellas **están**	they are

ser: to be

Singular		Plural	
① yo **soy**	I am	① nosotros/nosotras **somos**	we are
② tú **eres**	you are		
③ usted **es**		③ ustedes **son**	you are
③ él/ella **es**	he/she is	③ ellos/ellas **son**	they are

The next chart introduces other commonly used irregular verbs. Irregularities can take many different forms. Expand your knowledge of irregular verbs as you progress in your studies.

Irregular Verbs *Tener, Hacer,* and *Ir*

Subject Pronoun	*tener* to have	*hacer* to do/to make	*ir* to go
① **yo** I	**tengo** have	**hago** do/make	**voy** go
② **tú** you	**tienes** have	**haces** do/make	**vas** go
③ **usted** you	**tiene** have	**hace** do/make	**va** go
③ **él/ella** he/she	**tiene** has	**hace** does/makes	**va** goes
① **nosotros/nosotras** we	**tenemos** have	**hacemos** do/make	**vamos** go
③ **ustedes, ellos/ellas** you, they	**tienen** have	**hacen** do/make	**van** go

Tener (*to have*) is commonly used to state a person's age, and **hacer** (*to do, to make*) is often used in expressions relating to the weather. The verb **ir** (*to go*) will appear again in Part Two in the sections on verb tenses. It also appears in Chapter 6, Prepositions, since it is frequently used with a preposition.

Hint: Learn the irregular forms of verbs just like you would learn vocabulary words. It will pay off!

We have covered regular and irregular verbs that are stated as one word only. Single-word verbs are typically main verbs. **Estar** is the one verb that can act as a main verb when standing alone or as a helping verb when used with another verb. Let's look at **estar** in its role as a helping verb.

4.6 Spanish Helping Verb *Estar*

The following verb chart shows the forms of the helping verb **estar** with the verb form **nadando** (*swimming*), which is a form of the main verb **nadar**. These two verb forms combine to form the present progressive, which is covered in Part Two.

> **A form of the helping verb *estar*, rather than the main verb used with it, connects to the subject.**

Helping Verb *estar* with *nadar*

Singular

① yo **estoy** nadando   I *am* swimming

② tú **estás** nadando   you *are* swimming

③ usted **está** nadando

③ él/ella **está** nadando   he/she *is* swimming

Plural

① nosotros/nosotras **estamos** nadando   we *are* swimming

③ ustedes **están** nadando   you *are* swimming

③ ellos/ellas **están** nadando   they *are* swimming

Nadando is called a *present participle*. Its form remains unchanged and it cannot stand alone. It needs the helping verb **estar**.

Hint: Learn the concepts of helping verb and main verb. They will help you recognize which verb stands alone and whether a verb needs a personal ending or not.

As the term indicates, the present participle is used for a tense in the present. Spanish and English verb forms here are very similar. However, while their translations match, their uses are different, as you will see in Part Two.

4.7 Reflexive Verbs: Stating Names

Many beginning Spanish lessons include stating names by using a reflexive verb. For beginners, reflexive verbs are not easy to understand. However, a short introduction will help improve your understanding of these verbs. Reflexive verbs are used more widely in Spanish than they are in English.

We have used the verb **llamar** (*to call*) in the context of direct objects. Below we compare one such example using **llamar** to a second example using the reflexive verb **llamarse**, which is used when stating names.

When you are stating your name in English, you can do so in more than one way. You can say either *My name is Maria* or *I call myself Maria*. The English *I call myself Maria* is a more literal translation of the Spanish, which uses a reflexive verb. The phrase **yo me llamo** uses two pronouns, just like the English *I call myself.*

Note: **Me llamo** is often stated without the subject pronoun **yo**.

> **Reflexive verbs show an action performed and received by the subject. A reflexive pronoun is needed in addition to a subject pronoun.**

The next chart shows Spanish subject pronouns with their matching reflexive pronouns. Note that we only illustrate singular pronouns for now. Observe also the regular **-ar** personal verb endings.

How To State Your Name with *llamarse*

Subject Pronoun	Reflexive Pronoun	Verb	
① **yo**	me	<u>llam</u>**o**	I call myself Maria. My name is Maria.
② **tú**	te	<u>llam</u>**as**	You call yourself ⟨ Anna. / Charles Smith.
③ **usted**	se	<u>llam</u>**a**	Your name is ⟨ Anna. / Charles Smith.
③ **él**	se	<u>llam</u>**a**	He calls himself Andy. His name is Andy.
③ **ella**	se	<u>llam</u>**a**	She calls herself Kelly. Her name is Kelly.

> **With a reflexive verb, the first pronoun states the subject. The second pronoun, which also refers to the subject, is called a *reflexive pronoun.***

Me refers to the subject **yo**, and **te** refer to the subject **tú**, each matching its own verb form. **Se** is used with all three third-person singular pronouns: **usted**, **él**, and **ella**.

Se, the reflexive pronoun for the third person, could help you remember the verb family **llamarse** with its English translation *to call oneself.*

It is important to understand the concept of using two pronouns: You can omit certain subject pronouns, but you can never omit a reflexive pronoun.

! *Hint: Learning about verbs involves learning how to make matches between subject pronouns and verbs. With reflexive verbs, just remember to add another important pronoun match!*

Part Two shows you how verbs express time.

PART TWO: VERBS IN USE

4.8 Verb Tenses: Verbs Express Time

In Part One, you learned how to connect subjects and verbs. The term *conjugation* refers to the same concept, but also includes the aspect of tenses. In grammar, the term *tense* relates to *time.*

Verbs can express an action (such as the verbs **nadar** (*to swim*) and **comer** (*to eat*)) or a state of being (such as the verbs **ser** and **estar** (*to be*)). They also indicate when an action takes place.

The concept of adding personal verb endings was introduced in Part One. Now we will explain the concept of tenses.

Present, past, and future actions are illustrated below by Maria's experiences in Mexico and in the United States.

Maria is preparing for her trip to Miami. This all takes place in Mexico, where Maria lives. The calendar images are helpful symbols that will aid your awareness of time as expressed in three verb tenses.

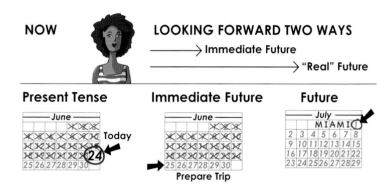

Let's start by describing what Maria is doing at the present moment—today.

Location: ═══ **Mexico!** ═══

Present Tense: What Is Happening Now
Maria, an exchange student, prepares for her trip to Miami. She plans to visit her friend Anna.

> **Verbs in present tense show an action or state of being at the *present moment*. This action or state of being is often habitual.**

Present Tense: *hablar* (to speak)

Mi madre y yo hablamos de mi visita.

- First-person plural present tense of regular **-ar** verb

- **Mi madre y yo** = we = personal ending **-amos**

My mother and I talk about my visit.

Singular		Plural	
① yo **hablo**	*I speak*	① nosotros/nosotras **hablamos**	*we speak*
② tú **hablas**	*you speak*		
③ usted **habla**		③ ustedes **hablan**	*you speak*
③ él/ella **habla**	*he/she speaks*	③ ellos/ellas **hablan**	*they speak*

Present Tense: escrib**ir** (to write)

Escribo una carta **a** Anna.

- First-person singular present tense of regular **-ir** verb
- **Yo**, the subject pronoun, is understood
- **a** = *to*, a preposition

I am writing a letter to Anna. (Literally, I write to Anna.)

Singular		Plural	
① yo **escribo**	*I write*	① nosotros/nosotras **escribimos**	*we write*
② tú **escribes**	*you write*		
③ usted **escribe**		③ ustedes **escriben**	*you write*
③ él/ella **escribe**	*he/she writes*	③ ellos/ellas **escriben**	*they write*

In the next example, Anna is asking Maria a question. The verb **tener** (*to have*) is used to state possession.

Present Tense: tener (to have)

¿Tienes tu pasaporte?

- Second-person singular present tense of irregular verb **tener**
- **Tú**, the subject pronoun, is understood

Do you have your passport?

Maria responds:

Sí, tengo mi pasaporte.

- First-person singular present tense of irregular verb **tener**
- **Yo**, the subject pronoun, is understood
- **sí** = *yes*, and **sí** includes an accent mark when it means *yes*

Yes, I have my passport.

Singular		Plural	
① yo **tengo**	*I have*	① nosotros/nosotras **tenemos**	*we have*
② tú **tienes**	*you have*		
③ usted **tiene**		③ ustedes **tienen**	*you have*
③ él/ella **tiene**	*he/she has*	③ ellos/ellas **tienen**	*they have*

The following example uses the verb **ir**.

Present Tense: *ir* (to go)

- First-person singular present tense of irregular verb **ir**
- **a** = *to*, a preposition

I am going to the United States. (Literally, *I go to the United States.*)

Singular

① yo **voy**	*I go*
② tú **vas**	
	you go
③ usted **va**	
③ él/ella **va**	*he/she goes*

Plural

① nosotros/nosotras **vamos**	*we go*
③ ustedes **van**	*you go*
③ ellos/ellas **van**	*they go*

The next two examples bridge the present and future tenses. All events expressed here are *about to* happen.

Location: ═══ **Mexico!** ═══

The Immediate Future: Upcoming Events

Maria makes a statement about upcoming events using the phrase *I am going to.* She expresses what will happen *soon.* The expression **ir** + **a** (*to go to*) followed by an infinitive indicates the immediate future.

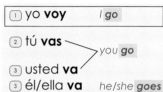

Voy a visitar mi amiga Anna.

   Conjugated   *Verb in*   *Personal* **a**
   Verb Form *Infinitive Form*
      ir + **a**
    *I **am going to** visit my friend Anna.*

- First-person singular present tense of irregular verb **ir** + **a**
- Infinitive **visitar**
- Personal **a** with direct object (a person)

The second example shows the same pattern:
(Subject) + Conjugated Form of **ir** + **a** + Infinitive.

Anna **va a hablar** inglés conmigo.

  Conjugated   *Verb in*
  Verb Form *Infinitive Form*

*Anna **is going to** speak English with me.*

- Third-person singular present tense of irregular verb **ir** + **a**
- **Anna** = *she* = **va a**
- Infinitive **hablar**

126

The immediate future is expressed with the present tense of the verb *ir* + *a* and an infinitive.

Review the conjugated forms of the verb **ir** with five different infinitives. Remember to include the **a** before adding the infinitive.

Verb: *to be going (to)* + Infinitive

Connect

Subject	Conjugated Verb	Infinitive
Yo *I*	**voy a** *am going*	**escribir.** *to write.*
Tú *You*	**vas a** *are going*	**nadar.** *to swim.*
Usted **Él/Ella** *You* *He/She*	**va a** *are going* *is going*	**comer.** *to eat.*
Nosotros/ **Nosotras** *We/We*	**vamos a** *are going*	**celebrar.** *to celebrate.*
Ustedes **Ellos/Ellas** *You/They/They*	**van a** *are going*	**visitar.** *to visit.*

Each conjugated form of the verb **ir** was used with a different infinitive: **escribir**, **nadar**, **comer**, **celebrar**, and **visitar**. Remember to include **a** before introducing the infinitive when using the immediate future.

The "real" future follows next.

Location: ⚊⚊ **Mexico!** ⚊⚊

The Future Tense: What Will Happen Tomorrow

Maria now expresses what she *will* do: *I **will** visit the United States, I **will** live in Miami,* and *Anna and I **will** speak Spanish.*

In both Spanish and English, the future tense is used to express an action or state of being that will take place at some time in the future.

Future Tense: *hablar* (to speak)

Anna y yo
hablar**emos**
español.

Anna and I will speak Spanish.

- First-person plural future tense of verb **hablar**

- **Anna y yo** = we = personal verb ending **-emos** added to infinitive **hablar**

Singular		Plural	
① yo hablar**é**	*I will speak*	① nosotros/nosotras hablar**emos**	*we will speak*
② tú hablar**ás**	*you will speak*		
③ usted hablar**á**		③ ustedes hablar**án**	*you will speak*
③ él/ella hablar**á**	*he/she will speak*	③ ellos/ellas hablar**án**	*they will speak*

Future Tense: *visitar* (to visit)

Yo visitar**é** los
Estados Unidos.

I will visit the United States.

- First-person singular future tense of verb **visitar**

- **yo** = I = personal verb ending **-é** added to infinitive **visitar**

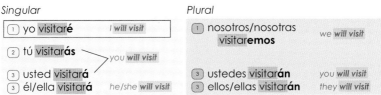

Singular		Plural	
① yo visitar**é**	*I will visit*	① nosotros/nosotras visitar**emos**	*we will visit*
② tú visitar**ás**	*you will visit*		
③ usted visitar**á**		③ ustedes visitar**án**	*you will visit*
③ él/ella visitar**á**	*he/she will visit*	③ ellos/ellas visitar**án**	*they will visit*

Future Tense: *vivir* (to live)

Yo vivir**é**
en Miami.

I will live in Miami.

- First-person singular future tense of verb **vivir**

- **yo** = I = personal verb ending **-é** added to infinitive **vivir**

Singular		Plural	
① yo vivir**é**	*I will live*	① nosotros/nosotras vivir**emos**	*we will live*
② tú vivir**ás**	*you will live*		
③ usted vivir**á**		③ ustedes vivir**án**	*you will live*
③ él/ella vivir**á**	*he/she will live*	③ ellos/ellas vivir**án**	*they will live*

Hint: Gray contrast boxes indicate that an infinitive is used to build verb forms for this tense, in this case, the future tense.

Hablaremos, **visitaré**, and **viviré** are examples of verbs in the future tense.

Here is a summary showing that future tense verb endings are added to the infinitive form in the three verb groups. For reference, you will also find a complete verb chart later in Part Two, with the verb **hablar** fully conjugated in four tenses, including the future tense.

Personal Verb Endings for Future Tense

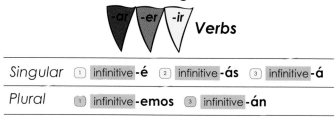

Singular	① infinitive **-é**	② infinitive **-ás**	③ infinitive **-á**
Plural	① infinitive **-emos**	③ infinitive **-án**	

> **The Spanish future tense uses personal endings added to the infinitive form. All three groups (-ar, -er, and -ir) use the same endings. Observe closely the use of accent marks.**

In Spanish, verbs in the future tense do not use a helping verb, such as the English helping verb "will" or "shall," to introduce the main verb. Instead, the future tense is indicated by adding special verb endings to the infinitive form of each verb, for example, **hablaremos**, **visitaré**, and **viviré**.

! *Hint: As you can see, early efforts pay off! Understanding the future tense depends on your skill to recognize a verb in its infinitive form.*

The next example takes place in Miami. Maria will talk about what is happening right now in Miami. Time is expressed with verb forms in present tense.

Location: 〰️ *Miami!* 〰️   **NOW**

Present Tense of *Estar* and *Ser*: First Impressions

A shift back to the present sets the stage for Maria's first impressions during her stay in Miami.

She describes where she is and how she feels, and she gives details about her American family, all using the verb *to be.*

Remember: Spanish has two different verbs—**estar** and **ser**—that correspond to the English verb *to be*. Context determines which one is used.

The chart below illustrates the different uses of **estar** and **ser**.

Use of *estar* (to be)	Use of *ser* (to be)
LOCATION	**TIMES AND DATES**

LOCATION

 Estoy en los Estados Unidos.

- **en** = *in*, a preposition with places, cities, or countries

I am in the United States.

Miami está en Florida.
Miami is in Florida.
- The name of a city is singular, matching **está**.

TIMES AND DATES

Q: ¿Qué hora es en Mexico?
- The noun **hora** is singular, matching **es**.
What time is it in Mexico?

A: Es la una en Mexico.
- **La una** is singular, matching **es**.
It is one o'clock in Mexico.

After 1 p.m., use a *plural* verb form.
Example: Son **las** dos.

STATE OF HEALTH

 Estoy bien.
- **bien** = *well*, an adverb

I am doing well.

PROFESSIONS

 La madre de Anna es maestra.
- **La madre de Anna** = *she*, matching **es**.
Anna's mother is a teacher.

MOOD

 ¿Estás contenta?
- **Contenta** refers to Maria, a female.

Are you happy?

 Yo **estoy** contenta aquí.
- **Contenta** refers to Maria.
I am happy here.

ORIGIN/NATIONALITIES

 Anna **es** de Miami.
- **de** = *from*, a preposition
Anna is from Miami.

CHARACTERISTICS

 El padre de Anna **es** simpático.
- **Simpático** refers to father.
Anna's father is kind.

> **Eres (tú), es (usted), somos (nosotros or nosotras),
> and son (ustedes, ellos, or ellas) all mean "are."**
>
> **Es means "is" with él or ella.**

Ser and **estar**, both meaning "to be," behave in much the same way as the English verb. Adjectives following the verb *to be* expand on the subject to which they refer. **Contenta** refers to Maria; **simpático** describes Anna's father.

The chart on the previous page includes several examples. Here is a short list of the basic uses of **estar** and **ser**.

Estar: Location, State of Health, Mood
Ser: Times and Dates, Professions, Origin/Nationalities,
  Characteristics

The verb **estar** can also serve as a helping verb. The next section explains how **estar** becomes a helping verb when used with a main verb.

Location: ～～*Miami!*～～   **NOW**

Present Progressive Tense: Around the Pool

What is happening at the pool? Relate actions of this *particular moment* to grasp the true meaning of the Spanish present progressive.

The present participle is a verb form that is expressed in English by verb forms ending in "-ing," such as *swimming* (with slight spelling changes) or *eating*.

> **The present progressive is formed with
> the helping verb *estar* and a present participle.**

¿Dondé están Ben y Andy?

Estoy nadando en la piscina.

Estoy comiendo aquí.

Where are Ben and Andy?

I am swimming in the pool.

I am eating in here.

131

Right Now

Estoy **nad*ando*.**

Helping Verb
estar

Present
Participle

I am swimming.

Right Now

Está **com*iendo*.**

Helping Verb
estar

Present
Participle

He is eating.

All regular **-ar** verbs form the present participle by adding the form **-ando** to the stem, as shown with **nadando** in the example on the left. All **-er** and **-ir** verbs add **-iendo** to the stem, as shown with **comiendo** in the example on the right.

> **The Spanish present progressive shows an action that is in the process of taking place. The action is not ongoing, as it would be in the English present progressive.**

Hint: In English, the progressive tense is used a lot. Become aware of how frequently you use a progressive tense in English. In Spanish, the use of a single verb form is preferred.

The following illustration shows four question-and-answer exchanges.

Location: ≈≈**Miami!**≈≈

Present Tense: Frequently Asked Questions and Answers

Maria visits Anna's school. Here are some of the questions her friends ask her, along with her responses.

Q1: ¿Cómo te llamas?
A1: Me llamo Maria.

Q2: ¿De dónde eres?
A2: Soy de Mexico.

Q3: ¿Estudias aquí?
A3: No, no estudio aquí.

Q4: ¿Hablas inglés?
A4: Sí, hablo inglés.

Note: The subject pronoun has been omitted in each question and answer on the opposite page. It is understood.

Let's analyze how these affirmative, negative, and interrogative statements are formed.

Forming Questions

Information Questions *Question word in first position*	Yes or No Questions *Verb in first position*
Q1: ¿Cómo te llamas? *What is your name?* *Question Word* Answer requires stating a name. **A1: Me llamo Maria.** *My name is Maria.*	**Q3: ¿Estudias aquí?** *Do you study here?* *Main Verb* Answer requires "yes" or "no." **A3: No, no estudio aquí.** *No, I do not study here.*
Q2: ¿De dónde eres? *From where are you?* *Question Word* Answer requires stating origin. **A2: Soy de Mexico.** *I am from Mexico.*	**Q4: ¿Hablas inglés?** *Do you speak English?* *Main Verb* Answer requires "yes" or "no." **A4: Sí, hablo inglés.** *Yes, I speak English.*
Information questions start with question words. Verbs usually follow next.	An equivalent for English "to do" is not needed to form questions in Spanish. Use the main verb in first position to form a question.

Making Affirmative and Negative Statements

Affirmative Statements *Subject in first position*	Negative Statements *"No" before verb*
Yo me llamo Maria. *Subject*	**Yo no estudio aquí.** *I do not study here.* *"no" in Spanish* *"not" in English*
I call myself Maria. *Subject*	In English, "to do" plus "not" and a main verb form negative statements. In Spanish, the word **no** is placed before the verb to form a negative statement.

Maria invites everybody to go to the pool with her. While at the pool, Ben suggests getting a snack to eat: Let's go to the food cart! This common command is the topic of our next section.

Verb Commands: Conversation at the Food Cart

Commands can be expressed in many
different ways. This introduction offers
two examples with short explanations.

English uses a simple command form
with the base form of a verb: "Eat with me"
or "order now" are two English examples. The pronoun "you"
is not stated, but understood.

Let's go and eat!
Eat with me!

¡Vamos a comer!

¡Come conmigo!

The first example above shows how Ben expresses a "let's" or
"let us" command based on the first-person plural of the verb
ir + **a**: **vamos a**. **Vamos a** can be accompanied by a verb in
infinitive form, such as **comer** (*to eat*).

The second example illustrates a request to Maria. When he
invites Maria to eat with him, Ben uses a familiar command
form. Spanish uses verb endings to differentiate between formal
and familiar requests. Familiar commands direct or request
someone—whom you address with **tú**—to do something.

Maria leaves Miami and is now back in Mexico. In your mind,
be prepared for events or descriptions of events in the past.
Shift from the present tense to past tense.

LOOKING BACK TWO WAYS

Imperfect Tense

Preterite Tense

Location: === **Mexico!** ===

Imperfect and Preterite: Reflections on a Recent Visit

Maria is back in Mexico. She reflects on her experiences in the
United States. To indicate that an action occurred yesterday,
or in some past time, we use the past tense of a verb.

Spanish verbs can express past time using either the imperfect
or the preterite tense. Maria's statements show three examples
of each of these past tenses.

Two Past Tenses

Imperfect Tense	*Preterite Tense*
Imperfect means not perfect, not completed. The imperfect tense is used for continuing past actions. Personal verb endings added to the stem indicate the imperfect tense.	The *preterite* tense is a past tense expressing actions that have been completed at a definite time in the past. Personal verb endings added to the stem indicate the preterite tense.

1 En Miami siempre hablaba inglés.

2 Mis amigos comían muchas hamburguesas.

3 Leía muchos libros.

1 Visité la escuela de Anna.

2 Escribí una carta a mi madre.

3 Viví con my familia americana.

1 – In Miami I always spoke English.

2 – My friends ate a lot of hamburgers. / My friends used to eat a lot of hamburgers.

3 – I read a lot of books. / I used to read many books.

1 – I visited Anna's school.

2 – I wrote a letter to my mother.

3 – I lived with my American family.

Spanish verb endings for the imperfect and preterite tenses indicate who performed the action. Each set of personal verb endings is different.

Imperfect Verb Endings

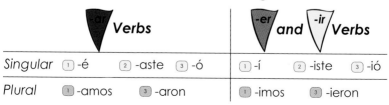

	-ar Verbs			-er and -ir Verbs		
Singular	① -aba	② -abas	③ -aba	① -ía	② -ías	③ -ía
Plural	① -ábamos	③ -aban		① -íamos	③ -ían	

Preterite Verb Endings

	-ar Verbs			-er and -ir Verbs		
Singular	① -é	② -aste	③ -ó	① -í	② -iste	③ -ió
Plural	① -amos	③ -aron		① -imos	③ -ieron	

135

Verb tenses represent a challenge to any beginning language learner. There is a lot to learn with tenses.

Learning regular **-ar** verbs is a key step in understanding Spanish verb tenses. For reference, we conclude this section with a chart showing the conjugation of the verb **hablar** in the present, future, imperfect, and preterite tenses.

hablar (to speak)

Subject Pronouns	Present Tense		Future Tense		Imperfect Tense		Preterite Tense	
	Stem	*Personal Verb Endings*	*Infinitive*	*Personal Verb Endings*	*Stem*	*Personal Verb Endings*	*Stem*	*Personal Verb Endings*
Singular								
yo *I*	habl **o** speak		hablar **é** will speak		habl **aba** was speaking		habl **é** spoke	
tú *you*	habl **as** speak		hablar **ás** will speak		habl **abas** were speaking		habl **aste** spoke	
usted/ él/ella *you/ he/she*	habl **a** speak/ speaks/speaks		hablar **á** will speak/ will speak/will speak		habl **aba** were speaking/ was speaking/ was speaking		habl **ó** spoke/ spoke/spoke	
Plural								
nosotros/ nosotras *we/we*	habl **amos** speak		hablar **emos** will speak		habl **ábamos** were speaking		habl **amos** spoke	
ustedes/ ellos/ellas *you/they/they*	habl **an** speak		hablar **án** will speak		habl **aban** were speaking		habl **aron** spoke	

The next two sections focus on two verbs that are useful for the beginning language learner: **gustar** and **hay**.

4.9 Using *Gustar*

Which do you like?

In English, you could state "I like hamburgers." In Spanish, this statement is expressed using the verb **gustar**.

Common English Translation:
I like the hamburger.

Me **gusta la hamburguesa.**

Verb (Singular) — Subject (Singular)

Subject (Singular) — Verb (Singular) — Direct Object (Singular)

(Literally, *The hamburger is pleasing to me.*)

Common English Translation:
*I like hot dogs **also**.*

Me **gustan los perros calientes** también.

Verb (Plural) — Subject (Plural)

Subject (Singular) — Verb (Singular) — Direct Object (Plural)

(Literally, *The hot dogs are pleasing to me also.*)

In general, the Spanish verb **gustar** means "to be pleasing to _____ (a person)." In English, the thing you like is the *direct object,* whereas in Spanish the thing you like is the *subject.*

Use the verb *gustar* in either singular form (*gusta*) or plural form (*gustan*).

To talk about something you like, if the noun is singular, as in the first example (**la hamburguesa**), use **gusta**. In the second example, **los perros calientes** is a plural noun, so it is connected to **gustan**. Later in your studies, you will learn about Spanish indirect object pronouns that are a key part of using the verb **gustar**.

The verb form **hay** follows next.

4.10 Using *Hay*

Hay means "there is" or "there are." Its form is the same whether it is used before a singular or a plural noun.

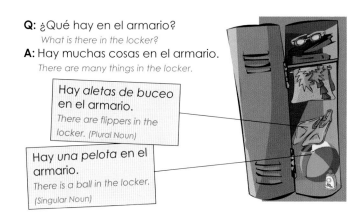

Q: ¿Qué hay en el armario?
What is there in the locker?

A: Hay muchas cosas en el armario.
There are many things in the locker.

Hay *aletas de buceo* en el armario.
There are flippers in the locker. (Plural Noun)

Hay *una pelota* en el armario.
There is a ball in the locker. (Singular Noun)

A thorough understanding of Spanish verb basics is essential before you begin the study of more complicated grammar. Be proud of your accomplishments—they represent the stepping stones to becoming a successful Spanish language learner.

4.11 Details About Chapter Sequence

The first four chapters in this book represent the core knowledge of basic Spanish grammar. Because you have reached the end of the fourth chapter, we include a short summary of the core concepts you have learned.

In the *noun* chapter, you learned the basic concepts of number and gender as they relate to Spanish nouns. Nouns are a basic building block of Spanish grammar.

La chica es americana.

The chapter on *adjectives* showed you how to add new words to the subject by using them to expand the noun.

You then learned how to take what you knew about nouns and transfer that knowledge to *pronouns*. Both nouns and pronouns can be used as subjects and objects to form sentences.

Jake ➡ he   Jake ➡ él

With a solid understanding of the basics in the pronoun chapter, you moved on to the *verb* chapter; you had established the necessary foundation upon which to add verbs.

In the verb chapter, you learned how building blocks— nouns and pronouns—are put to work. Verbs were introduced to combine with nouns. We call this combination of subject and verb a sentence, or *unit*. Understanding the subject-verb connection is a tremendous accomplishment. Your understanding of basic concepts allows you to link your knowledge of nouns and pronouns to the practical use of verbs.

In the process of putting different kinds of words together to form a sentence, you became increasingly aware of how words are used in a sentence. Consider this awareness your second great accomplishment.

You are on the road to success!

It is possible for a sentence to have only a subject—a noun or pronoun—and a verb. This is the essential framework of a sentence. The adjectives chapter is included in the core knowledge because adjectives expand nouns.

Verbs can be modified and expanded, too. As the grammar term indicates, *adverbs* ("ad-" meaning "in addition to") give essential information about when and how the verb's actions are carried out. It is a logical progression for the adverbs chapter to immediately follow your study of verbs.

You are now ready to begin Chapter 5, Adverbs.

4.12 Verb Grids for Conjugation Practice

Tenses

Practicing verb conjugation is an important part of developing solid skills in verb basics. In this book, verb conjugation is limited to the present, future, and two past tenses. Regular verbs express time through sets of personal verb endings, whereas irregular verbs have unpredictable forms. Personal verb endings for each verb tense are listed at the beginning of each verb grid.

Person and Number

The yellow and orange symbols that appear in each grid indicate person and number. Yellow symbols indicate singular pronouns, and orange symbols indicate plural pronouns.

How To Use the Grid

There are five grids that you can use for practice. To begin, select the verb you would like to practice conjugating. Write out each conjugation in the grid selected. For regular present and past tenses, fill in the stem of the verb before you add the corresponding personal verb ending.

The future tense grid has gray boxes to indicate that you need to fill in the verb *infinitive*. After you write the infinitive, add personal verb endings as they apply to the future tense.

PRESENT TENSE

    Regular Verbs in Present Tense
    Irregular Verbs in Present Tense

FUTURE TENSE

    Regular Verbs in Future Tense

PAST TENSE

    Regular Verbs in Imperfect Tense
    Regular Verbs in Preterite Tense

 **NOW**

Regular Verb:
A Pattern to Follow

Irregular Verb:
No Pattern to Follow

Regular Verbs in Present Tense

Regular 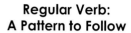 *Verbs*

Personal Verb Endings for Present Tense

Singular ① -o ② -as ③ -a   *Plural* ① -amos ③ -an

Selected Verb Infinitive _____

Singular Pronoun	Verb Stem	Verb Ending		Plural Pronoun	Verb Stem	Verb Ending
① yo	_____	____		① nosotros/nosotras	_____	____
② tú	_____	____				
③ usted/él/ella	_____	____		③ ustedes/ellos/ellas	_____	____

Regular  *Verbs*

Personal Verb Endings for Present Tense

Singular ① -o ② -es ③ -e   *Plural* ① -emos ③ -en

Selected Verb Infinitive _____

Singular Pronoun	Verb Stem	Verb Ending		Plural Pronoun	Verb Stem	Verb Ending
① yo	_____	____		① nosotros/nosotras	_____	____
② tú	_____	____				
③ usted/él/ella	_____	____		③ ustedes/ellos/ellas	_____	____

141

Regular -ir Verbs

Personal Verb Endings for Present Tense

Singular ① -o ② -es ③ -e   *Plural* ① -imos ③ -en

Selected Verb Infinitive _____

Singular Pronoun	Verb Stem	Verb Ending		Plural Pronoun	Verb Stem	Verb Ending
① yo	_____	_____		① nosotros/nosotras	_____	_____
② tú	_____	_____				
③ usted/ él/ella	_____	_____		③ ustedes/ ellos/ellas	_____	_____

Irregular Verbs in Present Tense

 **Each verb form is different.**

Selected Verb Infinitive _____

Singular Pronoun	Verb Form		Plural Pronoun	Verb Form
① yo	_____		① nosotros/nosotras	_____
② tú	_____			
③ usted/ él/ella	_____		③ ustedes/ ellos/ellas	_____

TOMORROW

Regular Verbs in Future Tense

Regular  *Verbs*

Personal Verb Endings for Future Tense

Singular ① -é ② -ás ③ -á   *Plural* ① -emos ③ -án

Selected Verb Infinitive _____

Singular Pronoun	Verb Infinitive	Verb Ending
① yo		_____
② tú		_____
③ usted/ él/ella		_____

Plural Pronoun	Verb Infinitive	Verb Ending
① nosotros/nosotras		_____
③ ustedes/ ellos/ellas		_____

Regular  *Verbs*

Personal Verb Endings for Future Tense

Singular ① -é ② -ás ③ -á   *Plural* ① -emos ③ -án

Selected Verb Infinitive _____

Singular Pronoun	Verb Infinitive	Verb Ending
① yo		_____
② tú		_____
③ usted/ él/ella		_____

Plural Pronoun	Verb Infinitive	Verb Ending
① nosotros/nosotras		_____
③ ustedes/ ellos/ellas		_____

Regular **-ir** Verbs

Personal Verb Endings for Future Tense

Singular ① -é ② -ás ③ -á   *Plural* ① -emos ③ -án

Selected Verb Infinitive _____

Singular Pronoun	Verb Infinitive	Verb Ending	Plural Pronoun	Verb Infinitive	Verb Ending
① yo		_____	① nosotros/nosotras		_____
② tú		_____			
③ usted/ él/ella		_____	③ ustedes/ ellos/ellas		_____

YESTERDAY

Regular Verbs in Imperfect Tense

Regular Verbs

Personal Verb Endings for Imperfect Tense

Singular ① -aba   ② -abas   ③ -aba
Plural   ① -ábamos   ③ -aban

Selected Verb Infinitive _____

Singular Pronoun	Verb Stem	Verb Ending		Plural Pronoun	Verb Stem	Verb Ending
① yo	_____	____		① nosotros/nosotras	_____	____
② tú	_____	____				
③ usted/ él/ella	_____	____		③ ustedes/ ellos/ellas	_____	____

Regular -er *and* -ir *Verbs*

Personal Verb Endings for Imperfect Tense

Singular ① -ía   ② -ías   ③ -ía
Plural   ① -íamos   ③ -ían

Selected Verb Infinitive _____

Singular Pronoun	Verb Stem	Verb Ending		Plural Pronoun	Verb Stem	Verb Ending
① yo	_____	____		① nosotros/nosotras	_____	____
② tú	_____	____				
③ usted/ él/ella	_____	____		③ ustedes/ ellos/ellas	_____	____

Regular Verbs in Preterite Tense

Regular  **Verbs**

Personal Verb Endings for Preterite Tense

Singular ① -é   ② -aste   ③ -ó
Plural   ① -amos   ③ -aron

Selected Verb Infinitive _____

Singular Pronoun	Verb Stem	Verb Ending		Plural Pronoun	Verb Stem	Verb Ending
① yo	_____	_____		① nosotros/nosotras	_____	_____
② tú	_____	_____				
③ usted/ él/ella	_____	_____		③ ustedes/ ellos/ellas	_____	_____

Regular **-er** **and** **-ir** **Verbs**

Personal Verb Endings for Preterite Tense

Singular ① -í   ② -iste   ③ -ió
Plural   ① -imos   ③ -ieron

Selected Verb Infinitive _____

Singular Pronoun	Verb Stem	Verb Ending		Plural Pronoun	Verb Stem	Verb Ending
① yo	_____	_____		① nosotros/nosotras	_____	_____
② tú	_____	_____				
③ usted/ él/ella	_____	_____		③ ustedes/ ellos/ellas	_____	_____

4.13 Spanish Subject-Verb Connection Practice

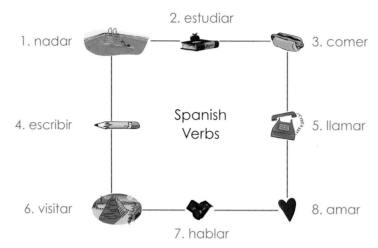

2. estudiar

1. nadar

3. comer

4. escribir

Spanish
Verbs

5. llamar

6. visitar

8. amar

7. hablar

Using the grammar person symbols, gender symbols, and English pronouns as a guide, complete the subject-verb connection for each verb given. First, write the correct subject pronoun in the space provided. Second, write the corresponding verb form next to each pronoun. Use the present tense.

Subject Pronoun	Verb Form	
1. ③ _____	_____	
you		
2. ② _____	_____	
3. ① _____	_____	
4. ③ _____	_____	
5. ③ _____	_____	
6. ① _____	_____	
7. ③ _____	_____	
you		
8. ③ _____	_____	

CHAPTER 5

ADVERBS

5.1 What Is an Adverb?   150

5.2 Adverbs of Manner   150

5.3 Adverbs of Time   152

5.4 Adverbs of Location   152

5.5 Adverbs Used to Form Questions   153

5.6 Details About Chapter Sequence   154

5.1 What Is an Adverb?

Adverbs act as modifiers. The prefix "ad-" in the word *adverb* means "to," "toward," or "in addition to." An adverb is a word that is used with a verb to expand its meaning.

read
silently

win
effortlessly

write
beautifully

swim
slowly

> **Adverbs add to or modify the meaning
> of a verb, an adjective, or another adverb.**

Adverbs can be easily identified. They usually answer the question *how, when, where,* or *in what manner.*

The form of an adverb is invariable; it does not change its form. Since an adverb does not modify nouns or pronouns like an adjective does, it does not have to agree in number and gender with the word it modifies.

Adverbs give information about manner, time, and location. Adverbs can also be used to form questions.

Let's start with adverbs of manner.

5.2 Adverbs of Manner

Adverbs of manner answer the question "How?" or "In what way?" Some commonly used English adverbs of manner are *slowly, quickly,* and *correctly.* English adverbs often end in "-ly."

Many Spanish adverbs of manner are formed from descriptive adjectives. These adverbs add **-mente** to the feminine form of the adjective.

> **The base used to form many Spanish adverbs
> of manner is the feminine form of an adjective.**

The following illustration shows how to form these adverbs of manner.

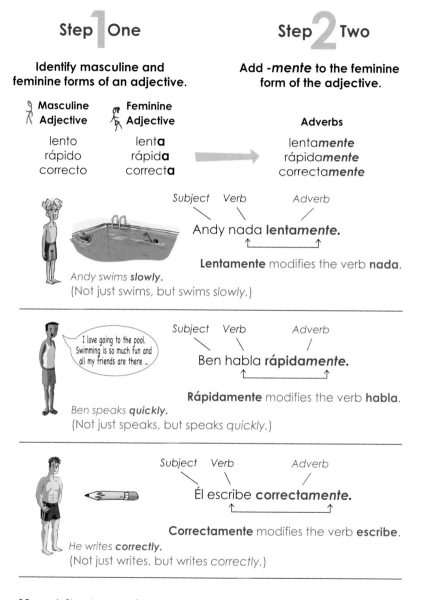

Step One

Identify masculine and feminine forms of an adjective.

Masculine Adjective

lento
rápido
correcto

Feminine Adjective

lent**a**
rápid**a**
correct**a**

Step Two

Add -*mente* to the feminine form of the adjective.

Adverbs

lenta**mente**
rápida**mente**
correcta**mente**

Subject Verb   Adverb

Andy nada **lentamente.**

Lentamente modifies the verb **nada.**

*Andy swims **slowly.***
(Not just swims, but swims *slowly.*)

Subject Verb   Adverb

Ben habla **rápidamente.**

Rápidamente modifies the verb **habla.**

*Ben speaks **quickly.***
(Not just speaks, but speaks *quickly.*)

Subject Verb   Adverb

Él escribe **correctamente.**

Correctamente modifies the verb **escribe.**

*He writes **correctly.***
(Not just writes, but writes *correctly.*)

Note: Adjectives with an accent mark keep the accent mark when they are used to form adverbs. See the adjective **rápido** and the adverb **rápidamente** in the lists above.

There are many adverbs that do not end in **-mente**. Among these are the irregular adverbs **bien** (*well*) and **mal** (*badly*). They are often used with the verb **estar**, as in the typical response to the question **¿Cómo estás?** (*How are you?*): **Estoy bien, gracias** (*I'm fine, thanks*).

5.3 Adverbs of Time

Adverbs of time indicate when an action takes place. Consider the following examples illustrating adverbs of time.

hoy (today) Present Tense	*ayer* (yesterday) Preterite Tense	*mañana* (tomorrow) Future Tense

*The party **is** today.*	*Yesterday you **ate** a lot.*	*Tomorrow I **will visit** Miami.*
Hoy refers to an action that is happening at the present moment. Use **hoy** with verbs in the present tense. The verb form **es** (verb **ser**) is in the present tense.	**Ayer** adds details to a completed action. Use **ayer** with verbs in the past tense. The verb form **comiste** (verb **comer**) is in the preterite tense.	**Mañana** refers to an action that has not yet taken place. Generally, **mañana** is used with verbs in the future tense. The verb form **visitaré** (verb **visitar**) is in the future tense.

5.4 Adverbs of Location

Adverbs **aquí** (*here*) and **allí** (*there*) indicate the place or location of a person or thing.

Let's look at the following examples.

Estoy aquí.

*I am **here**.*

Ben está allí en el vestuario.

*Ben is **over there** in the locker room.*

5.5 Adverbs Used to Form Questions

Some adverbs are used to form questions.
In Spanish, these are called
***las palabras interrogativas,* or question words.**

When adverbs introduce questions, they help you to identify the time, location, or manner of an action.

Cuándo (*when*), **dónde** (*where*), **adónde** (*to where*), **de dónde** (*from where*), and **cómo** (*how*) are commonly used to form questions. Note that all of these adverbs are written with an accent mark.

Each of the following examples begins with a frequently used question word.

Adverb as Question Word

When?	**¿Cuándo vas a los Estados Unidos?**
Time	*When are you going to the United States?*

Where?	**¿Dónde está Anna?**
Location	*Where is Anna?*

To where?	**¿Adónde va Maria?**
Direction	*To where is Maria going?* (Literal translation)
	Where is Maria going? (Common translation)

Miami!

153

From where? **¿De dónde es Maria?**

Adverb

Origin *From where is Maria?* (Literal translation)
Where is Maria from? (Common translation)

Mexico

To ask **where** someone is **from** in Spanish, always place **de** before the question word **dónde**.

How? Q: **¿Cómo estás?** A: **Estoy bien, gracias.**

Adverb   *Adverb*

Well-being *How are you?* (Informal) *I am doing well, thanks.*

When the question word **cómo** is used to ask a general question of well-being, remember to include an adverb with a form of the verb **estar** in your response.

What or How? **¿Cómo se llama usted?**

What is your name? (Common translation; formal)
How does he call himself? (Literal translation)

This concludes our brief introduction to adverbs. Expand your knowledge of adverbs as you progress in your studies.

5.6 Details About Chapter Sequence

This adverb chapter, like the preposition chapter to come, enables you to include more than a subject and a verb in your sentences.

In this chapter, we demonstrated how adverbs add to verbs by describing actions and states of being in more detail. In the next chapter, you will see how prepositions add to a basic sentence by expressing relationships such as time and place.

va al vestuario

You are now ready to begin Chapter 6, Prepositions.

154

CHAPTER 6

PREPOSITIONS

6.1 What Is a Preposition?   156

6.2 What Prepositions Express   156

6.3 Prepositions Expressing Direction and Location;
Prepositional Contractions   157

6.4 The Preposition **a**: Expressing Time in Questions
and Answers   159

6.5 The Preposition **de**: Expressing Possession and Origin   160

6.6 Verbs with Prepositions   161

6.7 Prepositional Phrases   162

6.8 Overview: Nouns and Pronouns as Subjects and Objects   164

6.9 Details About Chapter Sequence   166

6.1 What Is a Preposition?

This chapter deals with another group of little words you need to understand: *prepositions*. Just like adverbs, prepositions allow you to put variety into sentences by adding new information about time, direction, location, and ownership. Prepositions do not change form; they are invariable.

> **A *preposition* is a word or group of words that is placed before a noun or a pronoun to show a relationship in a sentence.**

Let's take a look at the kinds of information that prepositions can add to sentences.

6.2 What Prepositions Express

The following common prepositions show time, direction, and location.

a
at

a la una

a
to, into

encima de
on top of

en
in

en los Estados Unidos

alrededor de
around

Some prepositions can be used to express more than one meaning. **A** and **de** are common Spanish prepositions that are used primarily to express time or direction.

6.3 Prepositions Expressing Direction and Location; Prepositional Contractions

The prepositions **a** and **de** become part of a contraction when they are followed by a masculine singular noun. The preposition itself does not change. It simply contracts with the article **el** that immediately follows it.

Consider the following examples.

Prepositions Expressing Direction with Prepositional Contractions

Preposition *a*: to, into, toward   Preposition *de*: out of, from

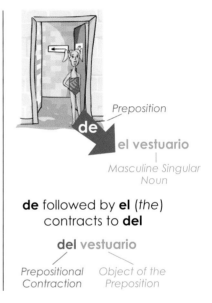

a followed by **el** (*the*) contracts to **al**

al vestuario

Prepositional Contraction   *Object of the Preposition*

de followed by **el** (*the*) contracts to **del**

del vestuario

Prepositional Contraction   *Object of the Preposition*

Only a masculine singular noun triggers a contraction with the prepositions *a* and *de*. The article *el* ("the") before a noun combines with *a* or *de* to form *al* or *del*. This new word is called a prepositional contraction.

The examples that follow use **a** and **de** with masculine plural and feminine nouns; no contractions occur in these examples.

❗ Hint: Are you becoming more aware how important it is to learn words with their gender? So much depends on it!

Prepositions Expressing Direction
Without Prepositional Contractions

Preposition *a*: to, into, toward   **Preposition *de*: out of, from**

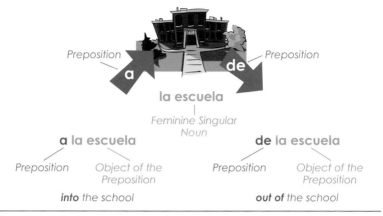

Preposition   **a**   *Preposition*   **de**

la escuela
|
Feminine Singular Noun

a la escuela   **de la escuela**
/   \   /   \
Preposition   *Object of the*   *Preposition*   *Object of the*
Preposition   *Preposition*

into *the school*   **out of** *the school*

Preposition   **a**   *Preposition*   **de**

los Estados Unidos
|
Masculine Plural Noun

a los Estados Unidos   **de los Estados Unidos**
| \ | \
Preposition   *Object of the*   *Preposition*   *Object of the*
Preposition   *Preposition*

into *the United States*   **out of** *the United States*

a la, a las, a los   **de la, de las, de los**
never contract   *never* contract

**A and *de* are the only prepositions
that are used to form prepositional contractions,
and they only form a contraction with *el*.**

*! Hint: Get into the habit of carefully examining the gender
of the noun you want to use with a prepositional contraction!
The article **el** meaning "the" gives you a clue.*

We continue with the preposition **en** (*in*), which is used
to indicate where something or someone is.

Prepositions Expressing Location

The preposition **en** is a common preposition indicating location. It corresponds to the English *at, in,* or *on*. The verb **estar** (*to be*) indicates a place or location and often takes the preposition **en**.

Where? — Ben está **en** la piscina.

Estoy **en** Miami.

Many prepositions expressing location have more than one word. For example, the prepositions **frente a** (*in front of*) and **encima de** (*on top of*) are multiple-word prepositions. If **a** or **de** is part of a multiple-word preposition, the prepositional contraction rule applies. When followed by a masculine singular noun, **frente a** becomes **frente al** and **encima de** becomes **encima del**. See Chapter 1, Nouns, for an illustrated example of **encima de** with a prepositional contraction.

6.4 The Preposition *a*: Expressing Time in Questions and Answers

The English preposition *at* has several meanings. *At* can express time as well as location. The Spanish equivalent of *at* is **a**. This common Spanish preposition can also express time.

Look at the following examples, starting with a basic question asking when Anna is swimming:

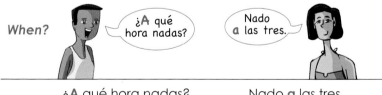

When? — ¿**A** qué hora nadas?

Nado **a** las tres.

¿**A** qué hora nadas?	Nado **a** las tres.
***At** what time (hour) are you swimming?*	*I swim **at** 3 o'clock.*
(Literal translation)	
When are you swimming?	
(Common translation)	

The examples above illustrate the use of the preposition **a** in both the question and the answer. You should become familiar with this pattern. Examples with other prepositions follow.

The preposition **de** also has many uses. There are several examples using **de** in Chapter 1, Nouns, and Chapter 2, Adjectives. **De** is used when talking about possessions and with the verb **ser** to indicate origin.

6.5 The Preposition *de*: Expressing Possession and Origin

Consider the following examples. When **de** expresses ownership, it means *of,* but it can be translated in other ways in different contexts. When **de** expresses origin, it always means *from.* Note that the example on the left uses a prepositional contraction.

Preposition *de*: Possession	Preposition *de*: Origin with *ser*
¿**De** quién es la toalla?	¿**De** dónde eres?
Of whom is the towel? (Literal translation)	*From where are you? (Literal translation)*
Whose towel is it? (Common translation)	*Where are you from? (Common translation)*

What Is Being Owned   **Owner**

la toalla   el chico
|
Masculine Singular Noun

de + el
of the

La toalla es del chico.
|
Prepositional Contraction
The towel is of the boy. (Literal translation)
It is the boy's towel. (Common translation)

De is placed *before* the owner.

Soy **de** los Estados Unidos.
I am from the United States.

When **de** is used in the question, **de** is in the answer. In a Spanish question asking about origin, **de** is always placed *before* the question word **dónde**.

As the examples above with **de** indicate, it is important to understand how one preposition can serve many different uses and have several definitions:

- **de** expressing direction = *out of*
- **de** expressing possession = *of*
- **de** expressing origin = *from*

! *Hint: Never expect a one-to-one correspondence between English and Spanish prepositions. Be patient when learning prepositions—they can be tricky!*

Verbs, too, like the company of prepositions. Next we will explain the meanings of prepositions when they are used with verbs.

6.6 Verbs with Prepositions

Hablar (to speak)

Let's begin this section with two English examples: "What are you talking *about*?" "Who are you talking *to*?" In these examples, the prepositions *about* and *to* add slightly different meanings to the verb *talk*. Similarly, the use of Spanish prepositions adds meaning to the verb.

Consider the following examples with the verb **hablar**. The example on the left shows the use of the preposition **a** in both the question and the answer. When using the preposition **de** or **a**, remember to use prepositional contractions when the preposition is followed by a masculine singular noun.

Hablar a (to talk to)	*Hablar de* (to talk about)
¿**A** quién hablas?	¿**De** quién hablas?
To whom are you talking? (Literal translation)	*About whom are you talking?* (Literal translation)
Who are you talking to? (Common translation)	*Who are you talking about?* (Common translation)

Hablo **a** Ben.	Hablo **del** chico.
I am talking to Ben.	*I am talking about the boy.*
When using **a** as part of the question **a quién** (*to whom*), include the preposition **a** in the reply.	When using **de** as part of the question **de quién** (*about whom*), include the preposition **de** in the reply.

Quién (*who*) is the question word used to identify people.
Qué (*what*) is used when asking the identity of things.
¿De qué? (*about what*) is used to obtain specific information.

Ir + a (to go (to))

The verb **ir** (*to go*) is commonly used with the preposition **a**.
When **ir** and **a** are used together, they indicate direction.

¿**A**dónde vas?	Voy **a** la escuela.
To where are you going? (Literal translation)	*I am going **to** the school.*
Where are you going? (Common translation)	

The preposition **a** is part of the question word **adónde**. Keep **a** in your answer.

Use this short summary to help you remember verbs with question words.

Estar (to be) (location)	*Ir + a* (to go (to)) (direction)	*Ser de* (to be from) (origin)
Where?	*To where?*	*From where?*
¿Dónde?	**¿Adónde?**	**¿De dónde?**
¿Dónde estás?	**¿Adónde vas?**	**¿De dónde eres?**

The next section takes a look at how a preposition and the noun or pronoun that follows are linked to the main part of a sentence.

6.7 Prepositional Phrases

Prepositions need the company of nouns or pronouns to form prepositional phrases.

> **A *prepositional phrase* consists of a preposition and a noun or pronoun that serves as the *object of the preposition*.**

Basic Sentence

Subject   +   Verb

Andy	nada.
Andy	*swims.*

Expanded Sentence

Subject	+	Verb	+	Preposition + Object of Preposition

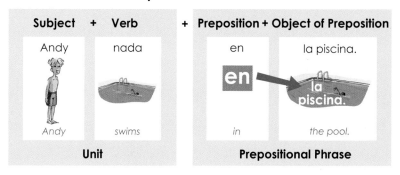

Andy	nada	en	la piscina.
Andy	*swims*	*in*	*the pool.*

Unit	**Prepositional Phrase**

The first sentence above, *Andy swims,* contains a subject and a verb. You could indicate the location—where he swims— by adding **en la piscina** (*in the pool*). The preposition is **en**. The noun **la piscina** (*pool*) is called the *object of the preposition* **en**. Together, the preposition and its object form a prepositional phrase.

> A *prepositional phrase* **is connected to the main part of a sentence. This connection establishes a relationship between the prepositional phrase and the rest of the sentence.**

A prepositional phrase is a *building block*. As a phrase, it is not able to stand alone, since it has no subject or verb. When you add the phrase **en la piscina** to the simple sentence **Andy nada**, you establish a relationship between the unit and the prepositional phrase.

The object of a preposition can be either a noun or a pronoun. How a pronoun becomes the object of a preposition follows next.

Prepositional Phrase with a Pronoun

In English, object pronouns such as *me, you, him,* and *them* can also be used as objects of a preposition. In Spanish, most prepositional pronouns are identical to subject pronouns in form; the exceptions are **mí** and **ti**.

> **In form, Spanish prepositional pronouns are the same as Spanish subject pronouns, except *mí* ("me") and *ti* ("you").**

Review the chart in Chapter 3, Pronouns, that shows prepositional pronouns using **para** as the preposition.

There are two special prepositional pronouns that derive from the preposition **con** (*with*). You already know that **mí** and **ti** are the two exceptions in form among the prepositional pronouns. The preposition **con** combines with **mí** and **ti** to form **conmigo** (*with me*) and **contigo** (*with you*).

Look at the following examples:

¿Nadas **conmigo**?
Do you swim with me?

Sí, nado **contigo**.
Yes, I swim with you.

This chapter concludes your study of the parts of speech essential to building a Spanish grammar foundation. Treat the following overview as a final step in assessing your progress.

6.8 Overview: Nouns and Pronouns as Subjects and Objects

A preposition is a word or group of words that is placed *before* a noun or a pronoun to show a relationship in a sentence. The preposition and its object—the noun or pronoun—form a prepositional phrase.

It is important to recognize nouns and pronouns in the different roles they play in a sentence: Nouns and pronouns can be used as subjects, as direct objects, and as objects of prepositions.

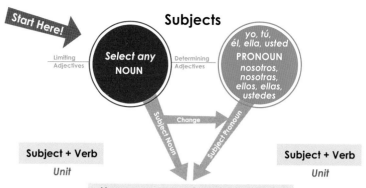

Subjects

Start Here!

Limiting Adjectives | *Select any* **NOUN** | Determining Adjectives

PRONOUN
yo, tú, él, ella, usted
nosotros, nosotras, ellos, ellas, ustedes

Subject Noun — Change — Subject Pronoun

Subject + Verb
Unit

Subject + Verb
Unit

Nouns or pronouns become *subjects* when *performing* the action of a verb.

Direct Objects

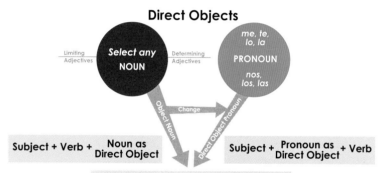

Limiting Adjectives | *Select any* **NOUN** | Determining Adjectives

PRONOUN
me, te, lo, la
nos, los, las

Object Noun — Change — Direct Object Pronoun

Subject + Verb + Noun as Direct Object

Subject + Pronoun as Direct Object + Verb

Nouns or pronouns become *direct objects* when *receiving* the action of a verb.

Objects of Prepositions

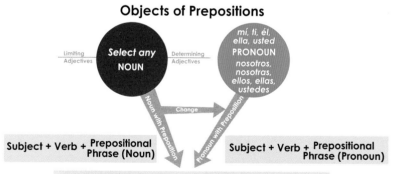

Limiting Adjectives | *Select any* **NOUN** | Determining Adjectives

PRONOUN
mí, ti, él, ella, usted
nosotros, nosotras, ellos, ellas, ustedes

Noun with Preposition — Change — Pronoun with Preposition

Subject + Verb + Prepositional Phrase (Noun)

Subject + Verb + Prepositional Phrase (Pronoun)

Nouns or pronouns become *objects of prepositions* when *following* the preposition in a prepositional phrase.

6.9 Details About Chapter Sequence

This chapter on prepositions comes after the adverb chapter for a reason. Your knowledge of the basic subject-verb connection should be strong by now, and this chapter, like the one before it, shows you how to expand that basic structure.

You are now ready to begin Chapter 7, Conjunctions.

CHAPTER 7

CONJUNCTIONS

7.1 What Is a Conjunction? 168

7.2 Two Common Conjunctions 168

7.3 Details About Chapter Sequence 169

7.1 What Is a Conjunction?

This is the final group of important words for forming sentences that we will study. The most common conjunctions will be introduced in this chapter: **y** (*and*) and **o** (*or*).

> **A *conjunction* connects words or groups of words of the same type.**

A *conjunction* is a word used to join similar elements in a sentence. These elements can be words, phrases, or sentences.

Beginning Spanish language learners start with the basic conjunctions we introduce below.

7.2 Two Common Conjunctions

Conjunction y (and)

Ben **y** Jake nadan.

| Conjunction

Ben **and** Jake swim.

In the example above, the conjunction **y** (*and*) joins two names. **Y**, the conjunction, expresses *addition*.

The next conjunction, **o** (*or*), expresses a different idea.

Conjunction o (or)

*Are you eating a hot dog **or** a hamburger?*

This example joins two words also. Here, the conjunction **o** expresses a *choice*.

The two conjunctions illustrated here are the two most basic conjunctions for a beginning language learner. Other common conjunctions are **pero** (*but*) and **porque** (*because*). Expand your knowledge of conjunctions as you progress in your studies.

7.3 Details About Chapter Sequence

Conjunctions are the last group of words that are important when forming sentences. The next chapter, on interjections, shows that interjections have no grammatical relation to other words in a sentence. As the last chapter of this book, it includes important final comments.

You are ready to begin Chapter 8, Interjections.

CHAPTER 8

INTERJECTIONS

8.1 What Is an Interjection?   172

8.2 Details About Chapter Sequence   172

8.1 What Is an Interjection?

For the children today: a free hot dog!

Interjections are sudden, interrupting words or phrases that are also known as *exclamations.* Interjections often function independently of a sentence; often they are not linked to a sentence at all.

8.2 Details About Chapter Sequence

The eight chapters of *Just Enough Spanish Grammar Illustrated* cover the basic components of a sentence, and therefore provide you with a general understanding of Spanish grammar.

In this book, often unusual ways of presenting Spanish language structures have been incorporated into the text. First, students are encouraged to learn each word with its matching part of speech. By doing this, you prepare yourself well for future learning! Second, illustrations make a fundamental concept in language learning come alive: recognition through context of the kinds of jobs that words have to do.

We conclude this final chapter with an illustration that shows four roles that Anna plays.

estudiante
amiga
americana
hija

Anna's Roles

Each time you place Anna in a different environment, she has a different role to play. In this way, Anna is like the parts of speech you have learned: Words have different roles to play in different parts of the sentence.

It is your turn now! Place yourself at center stage and become a successful Spanish language learner.

FINAL PROGRESS CHECK

Review the biographies from the "Meet the Players" page of the Introduction to find the answers to the following questions. This will test your skills on many of the topics covered in this book.

1. Which *noun* does the *adjective* **pequeño** modify? _____

2. Which *noun* does the *adjective* **inteligente** modify?

   _____

3. List three *prepositions*: _____ _____ _____

4. List two *direct object nouns*: _____ _____

5. List three *irregular verbs*: _____ _____ _____

6. Identify one *reflexive verb*: _____

7. List three verb forms indicating the ③ third-person plural:

   _____ _____ _____

8. Write the ③ third-person singular verb forms for the following infinitives:
   - a. ser _____
   - b. vivir _____
   - c. tener _____
   - d. amar _____
   - e. hablar _____

9. What verb tense is used in the biographies? (The calendar gives you a clue.) _____

   June — Today
   25 26 27 28 29 30

10. What part of speech is each of the following words?
    - a. lentamente _____
    - b. su _____
    - c. él _____
    - d. amigo _____
    - e. y _____

Nouns Adjectives Pronouns Verbs Adverbs Prepositions Conjunctions Interjections

174

Congratulations!

Dear Student,

In every chapter, we stressed the importance of taking what you learned in that chapter and applying it to the next. Use this same concept now, but on a bigger scale: Take what you have learned in this book and apply it to your future language studies.

Don't forget that learning a language is an ongoing process. It doesn't end when you close this book. In fact, it is just beginning!

We hope that this book has equipped you with the tools that will help you as you progress in your studies. We wish you the best of luck as you expand your knowledge of the Spanish language.

ANSWER KEY

1 NOUNS — Spanish Noun Practice

Practice One: Gender of Spanish Nouns
Masculine Nouns (M): 5
Feminine Nouns (F): 3

el bikini (M)
los anteojos de sol (M)
la pelota (F)
el salvavidas (M)
la piscina (F)
el traje de baño (M)
el silbato (M)
las aletas de buceo (F)

Practice Two: Number of Spanish Nouns
Singular Nouns (S): 6
Plural Nouns (P): 2

el sombrero (S)
la toalla (S)
las gafas de piscina (P)
el vestuario (S)
la silla de Susan (S)
los anteojos de sol (P)
el perro caliente (S)
el traje de baño (S)

2 ADJECTIVES — Spanish Adjective Practice

Practice One: Indefinite Articles
Masculine Singular Articles (MS): 3
Masculine Plural Articles (MP): 1
Feminine Singular Articles (FS): 1
Feminine Plural Articles (FP): 3

un perro caliente (MS)
unas cremas de sol (FP)
unas aletas de buceo (FP)
unas escaleras (FP)
una silla de Susan (FS)
un trampolín (MS)

unos salvavidas (MP)
un traje de baño (MS)

Practice Two: Descriptive and Limiting Adjectives
Descriptive Adjectives (Underlined): 3
Limiting Adjectives (Italics): 8

nuestro colchón de aire
una pelota
un niño <u>pequeño</u>
el sombrero <u>grande</u>
esta hamburguesa
la niña <u>bonita</u>
los anteojos de sol
sus toallas

3 PRONOUNS — Spanish Pronoun Practice

Dialogue 1: ustedes, tú; informal
Dialogue 2: tú, tú; informal
Dialogue 3: usted; formal

4 VERBS — Spanish Subject-Verb Connection Practice

1. usted nada
2. tú estudias
3. nosotros comemos
4. ellos escriben
5. ella llama
6. yo visito
7. ustedes hablan
8. él ama

FINAL PROGRESS CHECK

1. gato
2. perro
3. en, de, con
4. *any two of the following:* años, hermano, gato, inglés, español, hermana, perro, amigos, mamá, hermanos
5. tener, ser, estar
6. llamarse
7. hablan, son, se llaman
8. a. es b. vive c. tiene d. ama e. habla
9. present tense
10. a. adverb   b. (possessive) adjective   c. subject pronoun
    d. noun   e. conjunction

About the Author

Gabriele Stobbe, a native of Düsseldorf, Germany, began her professional career as a kindergarten and art teacher. Having decided to pursue proficiency in foreign languages, she lived in France and Spain for several years. Travels with her husband took her to South America and South Africa, where she began her undergraduate career at the University of South Africa in Pretoria, completing it at Duquesne University in Pittsburgh, Pennsylvania.

After years of teaching languages in high schools and for the Bayer Corporation, she formed her own company to provide language services and private tutoring in German, French, and Spanish.

A move to Washington, D.C. brought her prestigious assignments at the Goethe Institute, the Foreign Service Institute for the Department of State, and the Johns Hopkins School for Advanced International Studies.

Gabriele's lifelong passion has been to provide effective learning materials that will assist students throughout the critical early stages of their language learning. You may visit her Web site at *elingopro.com*.